US SAILING

MW00630278

THE CERTIFICATION SERIES

# Bareboat Cruising

## The National Standard for Quality Sailing Instruction

Copyright © 2019
Fourth Edition
ISBN 978-0-9741058-0-2

The United States Sailing Association

Printed in the United States of America.

Published by the United States Sailing Association
1 Roger Williams University Way, Bristol, RI 02809

**www.ussailing.org**
**www.sailingcertification.com**

# Acknowledgments

**Ray Wichmann** Author
At 30 years of age, with six years of college, no degree, and living on the beach in Hawai'i, Ray became a sailor. His first experience was crewing on a sail and snorkel boat in Kona, on the Big Island. This was followed by 10 years as an inter-island charter skipper. When he returned to the Mainland, he accepted an Instructor position at OCSC Sailing on San Francisco Bay and has been teaching there for 30+ years. He has sailed in Mexico, the Caribbean, and the Mediterranean, on boats ranging from eight to 150 feet, with one, two, and three hulls. He is a US Sailing Master Instructor Trainer, and a member of US Sailing's National Faculty.

**Richard Johnson** Co-Author
Richard learned how to sail at a coastal summer sailing program in North Carolina when he was 12. He can still name those responsible. After a few years in the Air Force, he answered a want ad for the Annapolis Sailing School branch in St. Petersburg and was there for over 30 years instructing and managing the branch. Several years as a charter boat skipper followed. He was part of the first group of US Sailing Keelboat Program Instructor Trainers, Basic Keelboat through Coastal Passage Making, and is a Master Instructor Trainer and member of the US Sailing National Faculty.

**Karen Prioleau** Contributor
Karen Prioleau directs the Professional Mariners Program at Orange Coast College in Newport Beach, CA. A lifelong sailor and professional captain, she has cruised all over the world, including a four-year voyage through Mexico, French Polynesia and New Zealand, as well as offshore voyages to Easter Island, Hawai'i, and Alaska. Currently, she is a Master Instructor Trainer for both US Powerboating and US Sailing, and chairs the US Sailing Keelboat National Faculty curriculum committee that develops training materials for US Sailing.

**Additional Thanks**
This book has been created by our talented team of designers, illustrators, photographers and writers. Bradley Schoch designed the page layouts. Management of this project was provided by Jessica Servis. Content and standards overview was performed by Pat Crawford. Photography provided by Peter Lyons Photography and Sunsail. Photo shoot location and boats provided by Club Nautique. Invaluable input and advice were provided by sailing schools, charter companies and volunteers, and there are a number of prior contributors to this book who deserve special recognition: Tim Broderick, Steve Colgate, Judy Durant, David Forbes, Rich Jepsen, Timmy Larr, James Muldoon, Tyler Pierce, Anthony Sandberg, Susie Trotman, and Dr. William C. Waggoner.

# Introduction to US Sailing

Since its founding in 1897, the United States Sailing Association (US Sailing) has provided educational opportunities for sailors at all levels of abilities — in all kinds of sailboats. The primary objective of US Sailing's education programs is to provide a national standard of high quality instruction for all people learning to sail. The US Sailing Keelboat Certification System includes a program of student certifications, a series of books, and an extensive educational and training program for instructors. It is one of the most highly developed and effective national training systems for both students and instructors, and is recognized nationally and internationally.

US Sailing is a nonprofit organization and is recognized by the U.S. Congress as the National Governing Body for the sport of Sailing in the Ted Stevens Amateur Sports Act. It has national training programs for sailors in dinghies, multihulls and keelboats. It is also the official representative of the United States to World Sailing, the International Governing Body for Sailing.

The US Sailing Keelboat Certification System is designed to develop safe, responsible and confident sailors who meet specific performance and knowledge standards.

The program begins with the Basic Keelboat certification level and progresses through Basic Cruising, Bareboat Cruising, Coastal Navigation, and on to Coastal Passage Making, Celestial Navigation and Offshore Passage Making.

With your US Sailing certifications and experience documented in the *Official Logbook*, you will have a passport to cruising and chartering boats both locally and nationally. Many graduates go on to confidently charter boats internationally.

*Bareboat Cruising* is intended to enhance your education. It was created to help you accelerate your learning curve and clarify your understanding of the concepts and techniques of sailing and cruising.

## What Makes Sailing Special?

The sport of sailing is open to people of all ages, incomes and abilities. Sailing offers virtually limitless choices of boats, each with its own unique characteristics, and the opportunity to explore a nearby cove or an exotic tropical location.

Most sailors will acquire entry-level skills quite rapidly. Mastering those skills is an experience that will be rewarding, exciting and pleasurable for a lifetime.

As you continue to sail, you will find that sailing is more than simply being pushed and pulled by the wind. For most people, sailing is meeting new friends, enjoying nature's beauty, challenges, and sharing a unique fellowship with all boaters. A tremendous camaraderie exists among sailors, particularly on the water, which makes sailing—and the people who do it—very special.

# Table <sup>of</sup>CONTENTS

# Chapter 1

# Introduction to Bareboat Chartering

Not very long ago, the only way to sail in exotic locations such as the South Pacific or the Greek Islands was to sail there first. Few people had the time, money, skill, and boat to undertake such voyages. However, in the recent past an entire industry has developed to put these fantasies within reach of anyone with US Sailing Bareboat Cruising Certification. With thoughtful research and planning, your entire family can enjoy the most fun-filled vacation ever.

## PLANNING MAKES THE DIFFERENCE

A bareboat charter provides you with the opportunity to sail a boat on your own in an area of your choice. As a vacation, a bareboat charter offers the thrill of using your sailing skills, exploring new or favorite waters, and spending time with friends and family.

Of course, any venture that involves moving people, supplies and equipment over both time and space requires planning. In fact, careful preparation for a bareboat charter can often spell the difference between a memorable success and a forgettable disappointment. At the same time, some spur-of-the-moment spontaneity adds extra spice to your trip. Having the basics covered, however, will ensure the foundation of a pleasant voyage.

**Destinations.** While you may not be able to reach all of the world's exotic ports on a bareboat charter, you can spend considerable time enjoying the Caribbean, the Bahamas, Mexico, the South Pacific, Australia, Northern Europe and the Mediterranean. Also consider destinations closer to home, such as California's Channel Islands, Maine's tree-lined coast and Florida's Gulf Coast with its barrier islands.

**Time of Year.** Many people charter to take a break from their local weather. New Englanders will head for the Caribbean, for example, to escape the winter cold. A trip to Northern Europe could be a refreshing break from a hot southwestern summer. Expect to pay higher prices during the busy seasons. Off-season bargains, such as summer on the sweltering Baja California Peninsula, may not be much fun at all. Your timing may be influenced by other weather factors and your competence to handle, for example, the 25-knot "Christmas winds" that frequent the Caribbean winter.

> " Those who get the most out of charters are the people who remain flexible, who are willing to change their plans on a whim or with the weather, and who believe that getting there is less important than enjoying the trip. "
>
> — Christopher Caswell,
> *Marine Journalist*

**Type of Sailing Area.** If you want to spend a majority of your time sailing, you might pick an area where anchorages are spaced far apart and offer a variety of upwind and downwind configurations. If you want to spend more time swimming, snorkeling, exploring or relaxing, consider locations such as the Virgin Islands where anchorages are within easy sailing distance of one another. Remote areas such as the Grenadines are beautiful, but they do not offer the bright lights of St. Thomas.

**Companions.** Sharing costs with another couple, family or friends may make a bareboat charter more affordable. Before doing so, consider some other questions: Is everyone compatible under close living situations? Does anyone have any special health considerations? Do you enjoy the same food and music? Do you want to appreciate nature on your trip or spend the evenings singing and dancing? How will you be sharing expenses on the trip itself? Plan a precruise tryout to get acquainted and answer some of these questions.

**Nonsailing Interests.** Many charterers seek to combine sailing with other activities, including shopping and sampling local foods. Snorkeling and scuba diving rank high for those going to tropical locations, and charter companies offer packages or contacts to make planning easier. Exploring ancient ruins, museums and monuments or simply mingling with people of a different culture can be rewarding. Planning becomes even more important so you have the right equipment and can target the best places for these activities.

**Skill Level of the Crew.** On your first charter to an unfamiliar location, you will need to factor in the experience level of the crew. Different charter areas pose unique navigational and sailing challenges including shoals, fog, proximity to shipping lanes and tropical storms. The British Virgin Islands offer predictable winds, short distances between destinations and easy anchoring. The Mediterranean, on the other hand, presents constantly changing wind patterns, crowded anchorages, and the challenge of foreign languages.

# A WORLD OF POSSIBILITIES

Each charter destination offers its own special aspects. You may have nursed a lifelong fantasy to loll on a white sandy beach in Tahiti or climb the ruins of the Parthenon. Advance research will inform you how to fulfill those dreams or where to go for new adventures. Travel books, boating magazines and charter company brochures are good places to start. Charter companies with first-hand experience can advise you on appropriate choices that suit your needs and experiences. Other sailors who have chartered can also be helpful.

If you have never been to your charter destination, there are a few factors to bear in mind as you plan your trip.

**Climate.** If you want hot tropical weather, aim for a spot near the equator, which is warm all year. As you head farther north or south, expect cooler weather with seasonal changes. Make sure that your trip coincides with a favorable time of the year at your destination.

**Experience.** Sailing skills are one factor in choosing your first charter. Will you feel comfortable handling the boat in the waters and winds of your charter area? Are you confident enough in your anchoring skills to sleep through the night? Consider also that you may be in a foreign country with an unfamiliar language and customs.

**Affordability.** In addition to the boat, your charter costs will include transportation, pre- and post-cruise lodging, food (on board and dining out), extra equipment, and additional supplies such as cooking gas, water, fuel and incidentals. To ensure a good time, leave extra room in the budget for the unexpected.

**U.S. West Coast.** The rugged Pacific coastline offers a variety of opportunities near the busy harbors of San Diego, Los Angeles and San Francisco, as well as coastal and island destinations such as the Channel Islands off Santa Barbara, CA. You will also find an abundance of protected waterways extending from Seattle's Puget Sound and the San Juan Islands north to the inside passage to Alaska.

**U.S. East Coast.** Good sailing waters can be found on the east coast from the southern tip of the Florida Keys to the northern tip of Maine, including the Chesapeake Bay and inland on the Great Lakes. The more northerly climates feature excellent summer weather, but you will want to go farther south to areas like the Gulf Coast in the winter.

**Europe.** The waters of the Atlantic around northern Europe and the Mediterranean present a wide array of sailing options. Most chartering takes place during the summer months. July and August in the Mediterranean can sometimes bring strong Meltemi and Mistral winds, but they are followed by excellent sailing weather in the fall.

**South Pacific and Asia.** Tahiti, Tonga and Fiji support an active charter industry. These islands enjoy a dry season with steady trade winds and occasional tropical squalls from early May to late October. Other areas, including New Zealand, Australia and Thailand, enjoy warm weather during North America's cold winter months.

**Caribbean.** The most popular charter area in the world, the Caribbean possesses many attractive features, including easy access from the United States and Europe, warm and protected waterways, safe anchorages, and a colorful infusion of cultures from both sides of the Atlantic. The Virgin Islands are ideal for first-time charterers.

Peak sailing season in the Caribbean runs from December through May, with steady trade winds from the southeast. Discounts may be available during the off-season.

## EXTRA COSTS CHECKLIST

- ► Restaurant meals, drinks and shopping
- ► Additional fuel, water and ice
- ► Moorings and dockage
- ► Guides, tours and scuba diving
- ► Customs, immigration fees
- ► Gratuities
- ► Local taxes
- ► Airport/marina transfers

## PREPLANNING CHECKLIST

- ► Make sure your charter trip coincides with good sailing weather at your destination.
- ► Match your destination with your sailing skills and your budget.
- ► Research the area you want to visit beforehand to determine where you would like to spend the bulk of your time and what you would like to do while you are there.
- ► Consult with charter companies for information about the locations they serve.

## COMPATIBILITY CHECKLIST

- ► Make sure there's enough room on board to allow each crew member some privacy.
- ► Don't mix smokers and nonsmokers or people with widely different expectations for the cruise.
- ► Include at least two competent sailors in case of an emergency. Encourage them to share their knowledge with others on board.
- ► Look for crew with mild temperaments and healthy senses of humor.
- ► Give yourselves a trial run with a precruise trip or meeting to verify your compatibility.

# CRUISE PLANNING

Planning is an integral part, and part of the fun, of any cruise. Like diners at a restaurant, you peruse the menu of options and select what looks most appealing.

Planning the cruise also includes some necessary details. You will need to factor in time to check out the boat before departure and time to clean it before you check it in at the end of your cruise. If crossing international borders, be sure you understand the procedures, have the necessary paperwork and flags, and allow time for clearing customs. You will want to know the sources (in English) of weather information for your cruising area.

When planning your itinerary, consider the desires of your crew. Your first inclination may be to cover as many miles as possible. For a group of hearty voyagers, this may be an ideal vacation. However, for those who want to visit cultural, scenic and historic sites, snorkel, read a book or, perhaps, just do nothing, a heavy sailing schedule will diminish their enjoyment. Think quality not quantity. Three to five hours of sailing a day is often enough. Sailing upwind or against the current can significantly increase travel time. Don't forget that most charter companies do not allow night sailing and strongly suggest that you reach your destination by midafternoon to be assured that there will be room for your boat. Check with your charter company to see if a one-way itinerary is an option. Resist the temptation to attempt too much; it is, after all, a vacation!

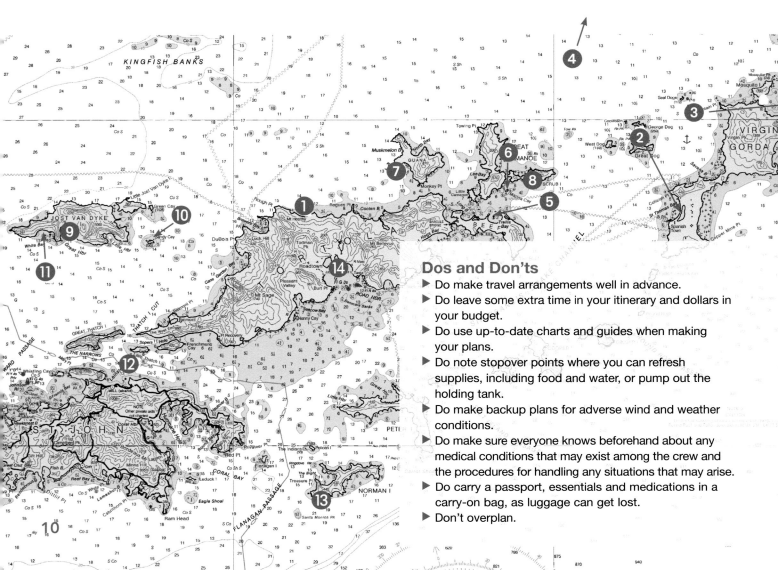

## Dos and Don'ts

▶ Do make travel arrangements well in advance.
▶ Do leave some extra time in your itinerary and dollars in your budget.
▶ Do use up-to-date charts and guides when making your plans.
▶ Do note stopover points where you can refresh supplies, including food and water, or pump out the holding tank.
▶ Do make backup plans for adverse wind and weather conditions.
▶ Do make sure everyone knows beforehand about any medical conditions that may exist among the crew and the procedures for handling any situations that may arise.
▶ Do carry a passport, essentials and medications in a carry-on bag, as luggage can get lost.
▶ Don't overplan.

# SAMPLE SCHEDULE

(Sample schedule modified from Sunsail 8-Day Charter)

**Day 1** Fly or take the ferry to ❶ Tortola, British Virgin Islands and check in to local hotel or directly to your boat if you have arranged a sleep aboard with your charter company.

**Day 2** **Morning** - check out boat, complete chart briefing and remaining paperwork, stow personal items and have lunch on board. **Afternoon** - sail 11 nautical miles (3.5 hours of sailing) to ❷ Spanish Town in Virgin Gorda. You can choose to make a day stop to explore The Baths on the southwest end of Virgin Gorda prior to reaching Spanish Town. Day mooring balls available at The Baths.

**Day 3** From Spanish Town, sail 9 nautical miles northwards towards ❸ Gorda Sound. Sail the length of majestic Virgin Gorda, where you will pass broad Savannah Bay before you reach the headland and enter Gorda Sound. Anchor west of Prickly Pear or grab a mooring ball in Leverick Bay for an evening under the stars.

**Day 4** Depart Gorda Sound and sail 13 nautical miles to ❹ the island of Anegada. Enjoy a prolonged spell of bluewater sailing as you leave Virgin Gorda in your wake and cruise through the blue to this flat coral atoll.

**Day 5** Enjoy a full day at the island of Anegada. Sparsely populated and teeming with wildlife, Anegada is a must-see for nature lovers. Anchor or secure to a mooring ball before exploring the island where you will find excellent snorkeling in Loblolly Bay, beautiful beaches on all sides, and famed lobster dinners ashore.

**Day 6** A full day's sail (19 nautical miles) from Anegada should take approximately 6 hours, arriving on the east end of Tortola. Here in ❺ Trellis Bay there is a small market for basic provisions and a bar for lunch. You can pick up a mooring ball at ❻ Marina Cay or anchor in ❼ White Bay on Guana Island. Scrub Island Resort ❽ is a short ferry or dinghy ride where you can enjoy an afternoon or evening in the infinity edge pool, restaurant, poolside bar, or spa.

**Day 7** Enjoy a beautiful 17 nautical mile sail from the east end of Tortola to ❾ Great Harbor (approximately 5 hours). Plan an unforgettable lunch break at ❿ Sandy Cay, where a spit of virgin white sand reaches out into the sparkling blue waters of the Caribbean. Following lunch, head over to ❾ Great Harbour. The mooring field here tends to fill quickly, so an early afternoon arrival is best. Spend the afternoon lounging on the beach in ⓫ White Bay, which is a short dinghy ride away. By night, enjoy sipping rum cocktails to the sound of live music back in ❾ Great Harbour at the famed Foxy's. Adventurous sorts can hike into the tall, rainforest-covered hills behind Great Harbour.

**Day 8** Sail the border between two countries as you navigate ⓬ The Narrows separating St. John from Tortola. From the mooring field at ⓭ Norman Island, a short dinghy ride will take you to the Caves for a beautiful snorkel adventure where many have hopes of discovering long forgotten pirate booty. (10 nautical miles; approximately 3 hours)

**Day 9** Return to base in ⓮ Wickhams Cay II - Roadtown, Tortola, by 11am, clean boat and debrief with the staff, take transport to airport or ferry dock to begin your journey home. (6 nautical miles; approximately 2 hours)

## HOW FAR CAN WE CRUISE IN A DAY?

If you assume an average speed of 5 knots for 4 hours, the daily cruising range will be 20 miles.

**D (distance) = S (speed) x T (time)**

**20 miles (D) = 5 knots (S) x 4 hours (T)**

If you are sailing into the wind or against a strong current, assume an average speed of 3 knots, which will reduce your range to 12 miles.

$$\text{Cruising Range (miles)} = \left(\frac{\text{Gallons of Fuel}}{\text{Engine Fuel Burn Rate (gal/hr)}}\right) \times \text{Anticipated Boat Speed (knots)}$$

# SELECTING A CHARTER COMPANY

As the potential customer, you will want to contact several charter companies. Look for professional practices and a business-like attitude at all levels of contact. Solicit the opinion of friends who have used the companies you are considering. Check references, referrals, and number of years in business. There are many issues to understand before you sign the charter contract.

Make sure you have a complete understanding of the financial arrangements. All charter companies require a deposit with your reservation. Your contract should specify the boat you reserved, the payment schedule, company refund practices, how loss of sailing time due to gear failure is compensated, and any additional fees. Most companies require a security deposit to cover damage to the boat.

Determine what is "standard boat equipment" and what is "optional gear." Such things as a dinghy with an outboard motor, barbecue, snorkeling gear, a sailboard or kayak, navigation tools, charts, cruising guides, binoculars and linens may fall into either category, depending on the company and the location. Understand what the costs are for any optional items you desire.

Some charter companies offer various packages, including the boat, airfare, transfers, lodging before and after the charter, provisioning, or even a captain, crew or cook. These conveniences may be worth the extra costs, especially if this is your first time "going foreign." Consider purchasing vacation insurance in case your charter is canceled.

# WHAT TO BRING

When packing, remember that cabin space is limited. Soft-sided luggage stores more easily than hard suitcases. The chartering life is very casual; bathing suits, shorts, T-shirts and tops are the norm for warm areas. Include a long-sleeved shirt, broad-brimmed hat, sunglasses and sunscreen for sun protection. Sandals and sneakers will protect your feet on rocky beaches. In cooler areas sweaters, foul weather gear, jackets and knit caps may be required. Bring one dressier outfit for dinners out.

To avoid offending local customs and religions, research what is considered appropriate clothing in various settings.

Clothes pins, resealable bags and rubber bands are very useful in the galley. Don't forget a few games, books and toys for the kids. Bring extra medications in case of travel delays.

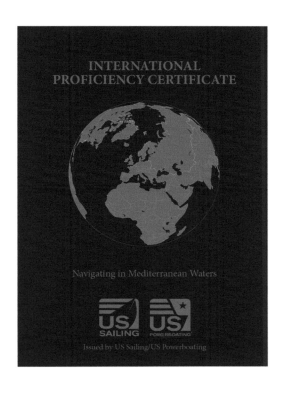

INTERNATIONAL
PROFICIENCY CERTIFICATE

Navigating in Mediterranean Waters

US SAILING    US POWERBOATING

Issued by US Sailing/US Powerboating

## DOCUMENT CHECKLIST

- ▶ Passport and visa
- ▶ ATM card, credit card and some cash
- ▶ US Sailing Bareboat Cruising Certification
- ▶ International Proficiency Certificate
- ▶ US Sailing *Official Logbook*

## INTERNATIONAL PROFICIENCY CERTIFICATE

This passport-style document is required for any U.S. citizen chartering in most European countries. It is available to current US Sailing members who have successfully completed the US Sailing student level keelboat courses through Bareboat Cruising Certification.

# WHEN YOU ARRIVE

Before you set out on your cruise, the charter company will verify your competence, usually by means of an oral quiz or, possibly, an onboard checkout. Your US Sailing Bareboat Cruising Certification and *Official Logbook* will facilitate this process. In many areas, you have the option of hiring a charter captain, which often makes the first trip easier. If the charter company questions your expertise, they may put a captain on board at your expense, but the charterer still retains responsibility for the vessel.

### Dos and Don'ts

- ▶ Do mark personal boat equipment that you bring on board.
- ▶ Do ask about unfamiliar gear or equipment.
- ▶ Don't forget that most charter companies manage privately owned boats or boats leased from individuals; treat their property gently and with respect.

Allow plenty of time to thoroughly inspect the boat and complete the checkout checklist to ensure it has all of the contracted items. Charter boats generally have a boat book providing charter company guidance and policies on boat equipment and systems.

# CHECK OUT THE BOAT

As the charterer of record, you assume legal responsibility for the boat. You agree that the boat is properly equipped and that all systems are in working order. You agree to pay (up to the limit of the insurance policy deductible) for anything you break, lose, or not noted as missing or damaged prior to departure. During the briefing and boat checkout, take notes of any discrepancies.

Charter companies routinely provide a skipper's briefing before you depart. It includes a chart orientation, suggested routes, anchorages, places of scenic and historic interest, areas that are off limits, and how and when to receive weather forecasts in English.

Ensure that water and fuel tanks are full and holding tanks are empty. Check the lights and fans in every cabin. Familiarize yourself with the operation of the propane stove and barbecue. On deck, be sure you understand the electronic displays, the reefing system and the anchor windlass. Check that there are sufficient dock lines and fenders. Many charter companies have an operations manual or "boat book" on board that includes information on the systems.

Make sure you know the location of emergency gear, through-hull fittings and fire extinguishers.

Check the ground tackle and get briefed on the safe operation of a windlass.

Review the boat systems, including engine operation, cooking fuel, and location of both the master switch and electrical panel.

# PROVISIONING

Meals and food can be very enjoyable parts of your cruising experience. Charter companies offer a variety of provisioning plans and menus, and each boat has a slightly different galley plan and equipment. For first-timers, the easiest approach may be to opt for full provisioning provided by the charter company. Alternatively, you can hire an independent professional provisioner. There may also be items that you will want to bring along or buy en route.

Lush pineapples in the Virgin Islands, fresh lobsters in Maine—these are part of the lure of cruising. Familiarize yourself with the storing, handling and preparation of local delicacies. Freshly picked produce will not require refrigeration, but fresh meat and dairy products will, especially in tropical climates.

If you are stowing your own provisions, carefully pack them in your refrigerator/icebox and in the reverse order of use. Stow the most frequently wanted items, such as ice water and cold drinks, in a separate cooler or in the most accessible location in the refrigerator. Freeze spoilable items such as meat and fish and place them in the bottom of a top-loading refrigerator.

If you provision yourself, unload and remove paper bags and boxes immediately, as they often carry insects or their eggs.

Make sure to keep perishables, such as lettuce, away from refrigeration cold plates. Always wedge opened containers with covers in an upright position. Fresh eggs need no refrigeration, but those bought from cold storage in the supermarket do.

## PROVISIONING CHOICES

Most charter companies provide complete provisioning and will go out of their way for special requests. Nevertheless, you may want to bring some favorite spices or herbs, a special brand of soda, or a particular bottle of wine which may not be available or may be prohibitively expensive in your charter area.

**Full** - usually means three meals per day plus a snack and some beverages.

**Split or Partial** - most often means breakfast, lunch, and afternoon snack, with some dinners ashore. Typically it will include three or four dinners.

**Custom or Individual** - food is selected from expanded menus and accommodates special diets and groups desiring different entrees.

**Basic** - includes only staples such as cooking oil, soap, paper products and condiments for self-provisioning or to complement your other selection.

Alcohol and soft drinks are usually extra, and their costs may range from cheap to remarkably expensive. Self-provisioning requires exact menu planning and sufficient quantities to satisfy your crew. Plan on large portions in cooler climates or longer passages and at least a half-gallon of drinking water per day per person.

### Dos and Don'ts

- Don't forget to ask about diet restrictions and/or allergies.
- Do keep cooking simple so you have time to play.
- Do review sample menus with your companions before your cruise.
- Do allow for dining out; sampling local food is fun.
- Do ask your charter company about ciguatera (fish poisoning) in locally caught fish.
- Do remove as much packaging as possible before departing the charter base.

---

### LOCAL SHOPPING TIPS

- Buy only what you can use immediately.
- Limit your purchases to food that can be peeled or cooked.
- Bring local currency in small denominations.
- Bring your own string, straw and reusable bags.
- Eating locally sourced foods will be kinder to your wallet.

Provisioning in foreign ports can be an adventure and a challenge.

# TRASH MANAGEMENT

You will need a plan for handling the trash that accumulates on board. It is best to follow the advice of your charter company, as they will know the local customs. Do not be surprised if these customs differ significantly from the recycling regimen you are used to at home. The International Maritime Organization (IMO) prohibits the disposal of all plastics overboard. Rinse food containers with salt water before putting them in the trash to help reduce odors and insects. Crush aluminum cans and remove both ends of tin cans and flatten the tube to reduce bulk. Bagging (or double bagging) in plastic trash bags and disposing of your trash ashore at your next port of call is common.

**Remember:** Plastic may never be thrown overboard!

# LIVING ABOARD

Living together on a boat requires cooperation, patience and a sense of humor. In close quarters, even minor habits can become annoying. Make sure everyone knows their responsibilities so no one person does all the work.

Keeping your personal gear in order is important in limited space. Use reusable bags to separate toiletries, jewelry, and other hard-to-find items. Pack clothes so the more frequently used items are on top.

## ONBOARD ACTIVITIES

While most charter companies schedule two or three nights ashore for dinner, the bulk of your evening entertainment will be self-generated. Part of cruise planning should include creative ways to spend your leisure time. Consider, for example, one or two theme nights with costumes and impromptu performances.

### LEISURE ACTIVITY TIPS

- Plan some activities for evenings and quiet times. For children, bring favorite games, books or toys. To save space, set a limit on how much to bring.
- Musical instruments are excellent for sunset concerts, but be thoughtful of other people's quiet hours.
- Books you don't have time for at home make for good reading on a cruise.
- Card playing offers many options for adults & children.
- Magnetic checkers, chess and backgammon travel well anywhere.
- A daily log or journal of your trip preserves your memories; school-age children enjoy this activity too.

### HOUSEKEEPING TIPS

- Dry wet items, including yourself, before going below.
- Wash off sand and salt water on deck.
- Run the shower water only to get wet and rinse off.
- Scrape and wipe down plates before washing to conserve water.
- Keep common areas clear of personal items.
- Clear away food and wash dishes promptly to avoid attracting insects.

#### Dos and Don'ts
- Do respect others' privacy.
- Do respect others' need for sleep if you are a night owl or an early riser.

### HEAD ETIQUETTE

- Sharing the head calls for courtesy and tidiness.
- Use the head as quickly as possible in case others are waiting.
- Empty and leave the bowl clean.
- Make sure the seat is down and clean.
- Wipe up water from countertops and clear hair from the shower drain.
- At night, turn off light before opening the door.

- Don't block a companionway by sunbathing or reading immediately in front of a hatch.

# PROBLEMS AND BREAKDOWNS

Every charter company wants to provide you with a carefree voyage. Nevertheless, you may encounter unexpected situations. A good charter company will have instructions and offer assistance when things go awry, whether it's simply starting an outboard engine or supplying you with a different boat. At the boat checkout, clarify what procedures you should follow. Be prepared and know what to do if you need help.

## HANDLING BREAKDOWNS

If items break or fail to function properly after a reasonable number of attempts, contact the charter company. In most locales, you will call on either a VHF radio using the designated channel or a cell phone. Be prepared to give specific information about your problem, what action you took, and where you are located.

| WHEN TO CALL |
| --- |

- ▶ Engine won't start or overheats
- ▶ Refrigeration malfunctions
- ▶ Head will not pump
- ▶ Dinghy lost or stolen
- ▶ Furling system freezes
- ▶ Anchor windlass doesn't operate
- ▶ Sails are torn or damaged
- ▶ Steering system fails
- ▶ Anchors or rodes are lost or damaged
- ▶ Through-hull fittings are damaged or inoperable
- ▶ Boat is taking on water

| RESTRICTIONS CHECKLIST |
| --- |

Charter contracts usually have a restrictions clause. Typical restrictions:
- ▶ Avoid unapproved sailing areas.
- ▶ Use only specified anchorages.
- ▶ Move your boat only during daylight hours.

### Dos
- ▶ Do clarify your charter company's definition of "emergency."
- ▶ Do try to problem solve before calling for help.
- ▶ Do note what radio channel or telephone number you should use to contact the charter company.

# RETURNING YOUR BOAT

Plan your return time carefully or you may incur additional charges. Have your crew packed and ready to disembark when you reach the charter dock. During the checkin, note any signs of developing problems. Many charter companies will send a diver to inspect the bottom. Their staff will also go over the sails, engine and other systems while you're still there. Any damage incurred during your charter will be deducted from your security deposit.

## CHECKLIST

▶ Remove all personal gear and garbage from the boat.
▶ Follow the charter company's instructions for dealing with unused provisions.
▶ Prepare a written list of damaged or worn equipment so that the charter company can fix it for the next charterer.
▶ Return logs, permits or other documents provided for your charter to the charter company.
▶ You should receive a receipt for all fees and charges from the charter company at the end of your charter.

Return your boat on time and in good condition so it will be ready for the next charter. Clean both below and above deck, including a fresh water rinse to remove salt and dirt. You should respect local water restrictions.

# Chapter 2

# Cruising Systems

Charter companies strive to keep their yachts well maintained, and problems with the yachts are uncommon. Should some piece of gear fail, you will not be expected to repair it yourself. The companies have well-trained service specialists to assist you. Often traveling on high-speed boats, they can rapidly come to your aid. However, if you understand how boat systems work you will be able to use them safely and properly, which will minimize problems. In the event of a breakdown, being able to clearly and accurately describe the nature of the problem is very helpful to these service personnel.

## ELECTRICAL SYSTEM

The boat's batteries and electrical system require careful management. There will be a master battery switch or switches which, in an emergency, can be used to shut off the entire electrical system. The bilge pump often bypasses this switch and is wired directly to the battery.

U. S. charter boats usually have a 12-volt DC system for operating the boat's lights, pressure water, radio, etc. In addition, there is a 120-volt, 60-cycle AC system that only works when plugged into shore power or if the boat has an inverter which changes the 12-volt DC current into 120-volt AC current. Foreign charter boats may have 24- or 32-volt DC system and 220-volt, 50-cycle AC system.

When you make your reservation, ask your charter company how your boat is equipped and plan to bring the necessary plugs, adapters, and converters in order to charge your various devices.

During your boat orientation, ask for clarification if you are unfamiliar with how to operate your boat's systems.

The electrical control panel distributes the power to different functions on the boat. The switches on the panel are normally labeled by uses. Typically, you will find the master battery switch, which controls the DC battery power, and the AC circuit breaker in the same area.

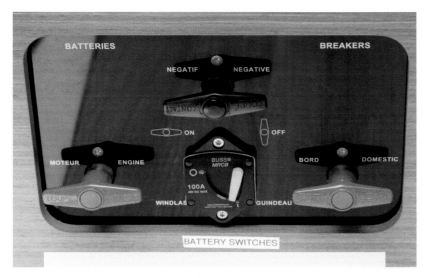

BATTERY SWITCHES

Most boats have house and engine start batteries switched separately. Sometimes these switches are in separate locations on the boat. The charter checkout briefing will cover the specific arrangement.

Some boats may have a single battery switch with four positions: 1, 2, ALL (BOTH) and OFF. Batteries 1 and 2 are used alternately as the "house" battery and ALL (BOTH) is used to start the engine.

## SHORE POWER CORDS

When hooking up the shore power cord, ensure that both circuit breakers (on the dock and on board) are in the OFF position. There will be a main circuit breaker (somewhere) as well as the master switch on the AC electrical panel.

Plug the cord into the boat first, carry a dead cord ashore, and plug it into the outlet on the dock. Turn on the circuit breakers. Remove the cord by turning off both circuit breakers and unplugging it from the dock first. Some charter boats have the boat end of the cord permanently attached, ensuring the correct procedure.

### BATTERY CHECKLIST

▶ Locate the batteries and check the fluid levels.
▶ Make sure the battery terminals show no signs of corrosion.
▶ Cables should be secure on posts.
▶ Check the master battery switch position before starting the engine.

### Dos and Don'ts

▶ Do monitor battery conditions using the voltmeter or amp hours meter.
▶ Do turn off electrical fixtures and instruments when not in use.
▶ Do run engine as directed by your charter company to charge batteries unless you are using shore power.
▶ Don't reposition the master battery switch with the engine running without first consulting your charter company.

# ENGINE MANAGEMENT

Nearly all modern cruising boats use auxiliary engines for propulsion as well as charging batteries for lights, refrigeration, radios and other systems. While these pages present generic information, engines vary greatly so it's important to adhere to the manuals and check out instructions and any boat books you receive for your charter boat. Informed operation and simple daily engine inspections will make your cruising more carefree.

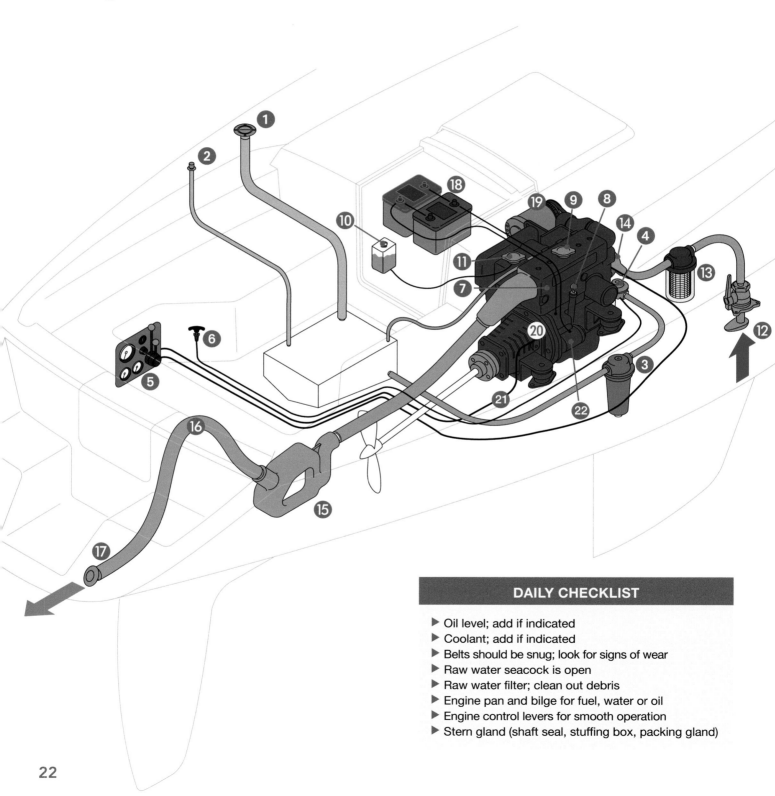

## DAILY CHECKLIST

- ▶ Oil level; add if indicated
- ▶ Coolant; add if indicated
- ▶ Belts should be snug; look for signs of wear
- ▶ Raw water seacock is open
- ▶ Raw water filter; clean out debris
- ▶ Engine pan and bilge for fuel, water or oil
- ▶ Engine control levers for smooth operation
- ▶ Stern gland (shaft seal, stuffing box, packing gland)

## Parts of the Engine

1. **Fuel cap** (deck plate) marked "fuel" indicates where diesel or gas should be pumped into tank.
2. **Vent** in fuel tank allows air to escape outside boat when filling tank.
3. **Primary fuel filter** collects impurities and separates water from fuel.
4. **Fuel pump** moves fuel into engine.
5. **Throttle lever** controls fuel flow.
6. **Engine stop control** (kill lever/switch) turns off fuel flow to engine.
7. **Engine block** houses cylinders and fuel injectors (diesel) or spark plugs (gasoline).
8. **Oil dipstick** indicates quantity and condition of oil.
9. **Oil filler cap** allows addition of oil when indicated on dipstick.
10. **Coolant reservoir** stores excess coolant fluid until required.
11. **Coolant cap** allows addition of water or coolant if there is no header tank.
12. **Seacock** lets raw water flow in.
13. **Raw water strainer** filters and collects debris.
14. **Raw water intake system** includes pump with rubber impeller that circulates seawater to cool engine and exhaust gases.
15. **Lift can** helps to prevent water backflow into engine.
16. **High loop** also helps prevent water backflow into engine.
17. **Exhaust outlet** is working properly when water flows out. If there is no water, turn off engine immediately and check raw water intake system. Make sure seacock is open and filter is clean. Check pump impeller.
18. **Batteries** provide electricity for lights, instruments, starting engine and, on some boats, refrigeration.
19. **Alternator** generates electricity to charge batteries.
20. **Transmission** transfers engine power to propeller shaft and changes its direction to forward, reverse or neutral.
21. **Linkage** connects lever controls to transmission.
22. **Starter motor** turns flywheel to start engine.

## Starting Procedure

1. Check the boat book or manuals to determine what steps are appropriate.
2. Complete daily checklist.
3. Turn battery switch to correct setting.
4. Engage engine blower (when available).
5. Put engine stop control in RUN position (when present).
6. Put gear shift in NEUTRAL, open throttle slightly.
7. Preheat with glow-plug control (if equipped) for 10-30 seconds.
8. Turn on ignition (oil pressure alarm should sound) and start engine.
9. Throttle engine to steady idle (oil pressure alarm should stop).
10. Check exhaust for consistent water flow.
11. Check gauges (oil pressure, water temperature, ammeter).

## Stopping Procedure

1. Check the boat book or manuals to determine what steps are appropriate.
2. Throttle to idle.
3. Shift to NEUTRAL.
4. Put the engine stop control in STOP position.
5. Return engine stop control to RUN position after engine stops.
6. Turn ignition key to OFF position.

**NOTE:** Put transmission in REVERSE while sailing to prevent shaft from spinning.

# VENTILATION

In warm climates, your comfort below deck will often depend upon adequate ventilation. Underway, you will usually keep hatches and ports closed to prevent spray going below. Once anchored, open up your boat to refresh and cool the cabin.

**Wind scoop is a cloth funnel suspended from the jib halyard and forestay to direct air into the forepeak.**

**Hatches should be latched open to permit free flow of air through the boat.**

**Dorade cowls permit air to enter and exit below decks.**

**Stern cowls ventilate the aft sections of the boat.**

**Ports allow ventilation.**

## VENTILATION TIPS

**When Anchored:**
▶ Open all ports and hatches to increase airflow.
▶ Suspend the wind scoop in the forward hatch.
▶ Position cowls on Dorade to intake and expel air.
▶ 12-volt fans draw considerable power.
▶ Monitor battery condition.

A properly designed Dorade allows the cowl to face forward for ventilation and prevent spray from going below while underway. Face cowls aft if water enters the cabin.

While anchored or docked, open all ports to allow fresh air into the boat. If you leave the boat unattended, close ports to avoid theft or rainwater.

Secure ports while underway to prevent spray intrusion below. Both dogs (latches) should be tightened equally. Do not overtighten.

# FRESH WATER

Charter boats carry a limited amount of fresh water and, in many locations, there is a charge for refilling. Familiarize yourself with the water system in the galley, head(s) and ondeck shower(s). The pressure to produce a continuous flow of water relies on battery power, so caution everyone to turn off unused faucets and valves. When everyone has turned in for the night, turn off the fresh water pump at the electrical panel. Some boats have manual water pumps in the head and galley that may be hand- or foot-operated.

## FRESH WATER CHECKLIST

▶ Locate filler deck plate and control valves for water tanks.
▶ Turn off water pressure switch when everyone has retired for the night and when the boat is left unattended.
▶ Close valves and faucets when not in use.
▶ Use the manifold valves to ensure that you draw from only one tank at a time.

Regularly check water level.

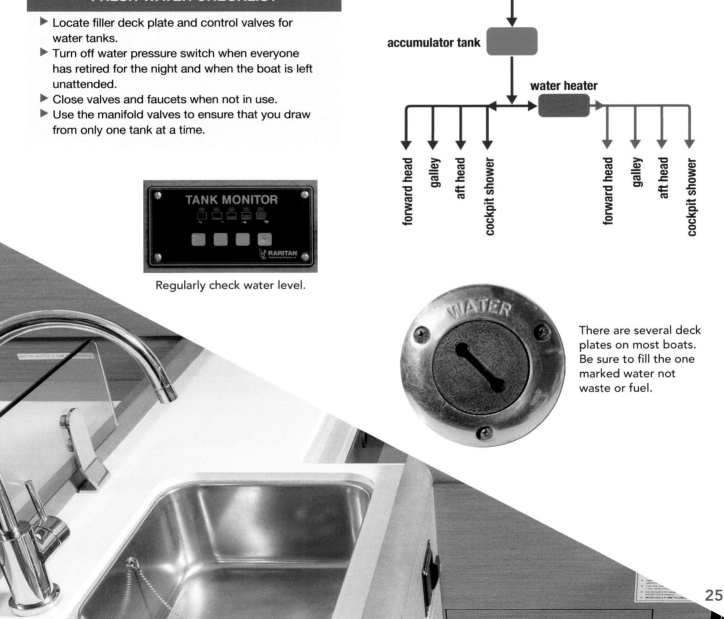

There are several deck plates on most boats. Be sure to fill the one marked water not waste or fuel.

# HEAD

In order to prevent clogging or breakdown of this critical system, whether manual or electric, brief everyone on the operation of the head and the use of the holding tank. The head is designed to handle human waste, small amounts of toilet paper and nothing else. Ask your charter company about disposal regulations in your charter area and locations of pumpout stations. Since several people may share a head, tidying the area is important.

## HEAD OPERATION PROCEDURE

1. Open raw water seacock.
2. Open valve to holding tank or discharge seacock as required.
3. Depress hand or foot lever and pump a small amount of water into bowl before using.
4. Depress hand or foot lever to flush, and pump until bowl is clear. Pump additional strokes to ensure discharge line is clear.
5. Release hand or foot lever and pump bowl dry.
6. Close all valves, seacock(s) and lid after use.

## Dos and Don'ts

▶ Do make sure everyone knows how to use the head properly before leaving the dock.
▶ Don't continue pumping when you encounter resistance.
▶ Do open all valves and seacock(s) before and close after using the head.
▶ Do use marine toilet paper.
▶ Do monitor water usage if your head uses fresh water.

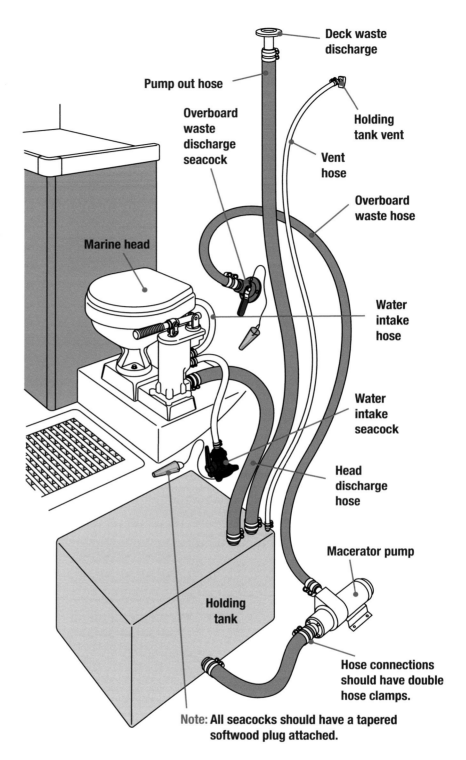

Deck waste discharge

Pump out hose

Overboard waste discharge seacock

Holding tank vent

Vent hose

Overboard waste hose

Marine head

Water intake hose

Water intake seacock

Head discharge hose

Macerator pump

Holding tank

Hose connections should have double hose clamps.

Note: **All seacocks should have a tapered softwood plug attached.**

**NOTE:** In U.S. waters, untreated sewage cannot be discharged overboard within three miles of the Atlantic and Pacific coasts, and within nine miles of the Gulf coast. In other countries the rules may be more lenient; however, it is common courtesy to use your holding tanks while in anchorages, harbors and marinas. If there are no pumpout facilities (check with your charter company), empty your holding tank(s) while sailing in open water between overnight stops.

# BILGE AND THROUGH-HULL SYSTEMS

Check out the bilge system carefully when reviewing the boat with the charter company. Test the operation of all bilge pumps and ask what is normal bilge water before accepting the charter boat. Draining iceboxes and certain types of stern glands will produce some bilge water during normal operation. The charter company may direct you to close all galley and head through-hulls when underway.

## BILGE CHECKLIST

► By lifting the float switch when the main battery switch is turned off, determine whether or not the automatic bilge pump switch bypasses the main battery switch and goes directly to the battery. The pump will start unless it's wired through the main battery switch.
► Locate and operate each through-hull valve.
► Check intake screens regularly.
► Clear debris from bilge that would lodge in float switch.
► Monitor automatic pump if it does not have an alarm. Continuous operation indicates trouble.

Keep intake screen free of debris to prevent clogging the bilge pump. A float switch activates the automatic bilge pump. A clogged switch will cause the pump to run continuously and burn out.

Locate and test the operation of the manual bilge pump.

If there is no diagram of the through-hull fittings and bilge pump locations, make one of your own (see illustration).

Each through-hull fitting should be labeled. Wooden plugs (often stored with the other emergency gear) should be available with sizes for each through-hull.

- For easy access, store provisions in the reverse order of planned consumption.
- Provisions may shift while underway, so be careful when opening lockers both during and after a sail.
- Wear shoes when cooking underway and avoid wearing long sleeves or flowing garments.
- Tossing food scraps overboard may be inappropriate or illegal in some areas.
- Be cautious regarding sanitation and food temperatures. Tropical sun is hot and food poisoning unpleasant.
- Prepare snacks ahead and have them easily accessible while sailing.
- Consider foods with ginger such as ginger snaps or ginger ale to settle stomachs.

# GALLEY

A happy cruise relies on a good galley. Refrigeration, stoves with ovens, and pressurized water make cooking easy and convenient. Refrigeration requires power, so the engine will need to be run daily in order to charge the batteries or to run a belt-driven, compressor-type refrigerator. Optional equipment often includes barbecues for outdoor cooking and ice chests for warm climates.

**Galley lockers should be fastened securely when underway. Stow heavy items such as canned goods and pots as low as possible. Towers of canned goods in any locker may shift and fall.**

**Top-loading refrigerators and iceboxes stay colder longer than front-opening models. To keep the cold in, minimize opening the icebox by removing all meal ingredients at the same time.**

**Gimbals should be unlocked only when cooking underway.**

## STOVES

The standard on charter boats is a propane stove, with three or four burners and an oven. They are efficient and easy to use. However, because propane is heavier than air, it will flow into the bilge if allowed to leak into the boat. The charter company should demonstrate the correct operating procedure during the boat checkout. Ask if they don't.

**NOTE:** Watch children carefully around the stove. If the gimbals are unlocked, a curious child may pull on the stove, causing pots and their contents to spill. Opening the oven door may also upset the balance of the stove.

**Solenoid Switch**

## SOLENOID SWITCH

For safety and convenience, a solenoid is installed to shut off the propane at the tank. The switch that controls it is usually located near the stove or on the electrical panel and labled LPG. If the stove doesn't light, be sure the solenoid is open. In the event of a fire, there are three places to stop the flow of fuel: the stove; the solenoid switch; and the propane tank.

### STOVE OPERATION

1 Ensure the tank valve is open and turn on the solenoid.

2 Strike the match or starter before turning on the burner control.

3 When you finish all cooking, first turn off the solenoid. When the flame goes out, turn off the burner(s), and close the tank valve.

4 Check that all stove/ oven controls are off and relock the gimbals.

PROPANE SWITCH

### Dos and Don'ts

▶ Do check the location of shut-off valves, electrical breakers and solenoid switches.

▶ Do locate the fire extinguisher and the fire blanket (if there is one).

▶ Do shut off the stove fuel supply when not in use.

▶ Don't leave the burner and oven controls on after turning off the fuel supply.

▶ Don't forget to close the tank valves when leaving the boat.

# SAFETY

Safety plays an important role in the success of your cruise. Avoid accidents by using safety gear, exercising caution around fire, protecting yourself from the sun, and following other safety guidelines. Familiarize yourself thoroughly with the location of safety gear, how to use it, and the quickest way out from down below. Ensure that the crew knows how to make an emergency call using the boat's radio.

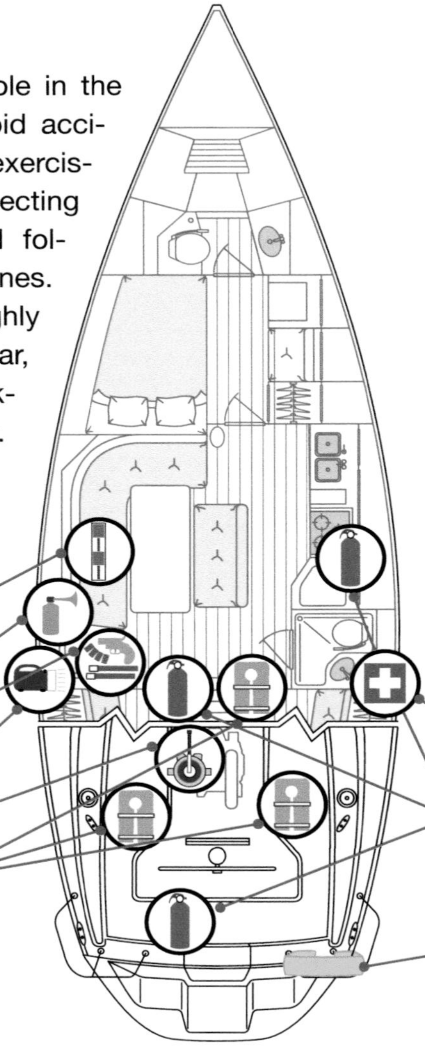

Radar reflector
Horn
Flares
Flashlight
Manual bilge pump
Life jackets and harnesses are frequently located in the cockpit locker or below near the companionway.
First aid kit
Fire extinguishers are located near the galley, the engine compartment and the cockpit. On big boats, you will often find them near a forward hatch as well.
Rescue sling and horseshoe rings are often mounted on the transom or stern pulpit.


## SAFETY EQUIPMENT CHECKLIST

The charter customer is responsible for ensuring that the required gear is on board.

**Before leaving the dock:**

- Locate all fire extinguishers.
- Try on life jackets and harnesses.
- Know how to use EPIRB, flares, and other safety gear.
- Know how to use VHF radio.
- Make sure the bitter end of the rescue sling line is fastened to the boat.
- Know how to use crew overboard equipment.

**Once underway:**

- Practice an overboard rescue using a float.

## SUN PROTECTION

Prolonged sun exposure causes sunburn and contributes to the development of skin cancer. Wear sunblock, broad-brimmed hats and long-sleeved, lightweight shirts to protect yourself. Good sunglasses protect your eyes from glare and harmful ultraviolet rays. Avoid direct sun, especially between 10 a.m. and 4 p.m. To reduce the chance of heat exhaustion or heat stroke, don't overexert yourself and drink plenty of water, even if you are in the shade.

SPF 30
BARE REPUBLIC
NATURAL MINERAL SUNSCREEN
41.6511°N
71.2595°W

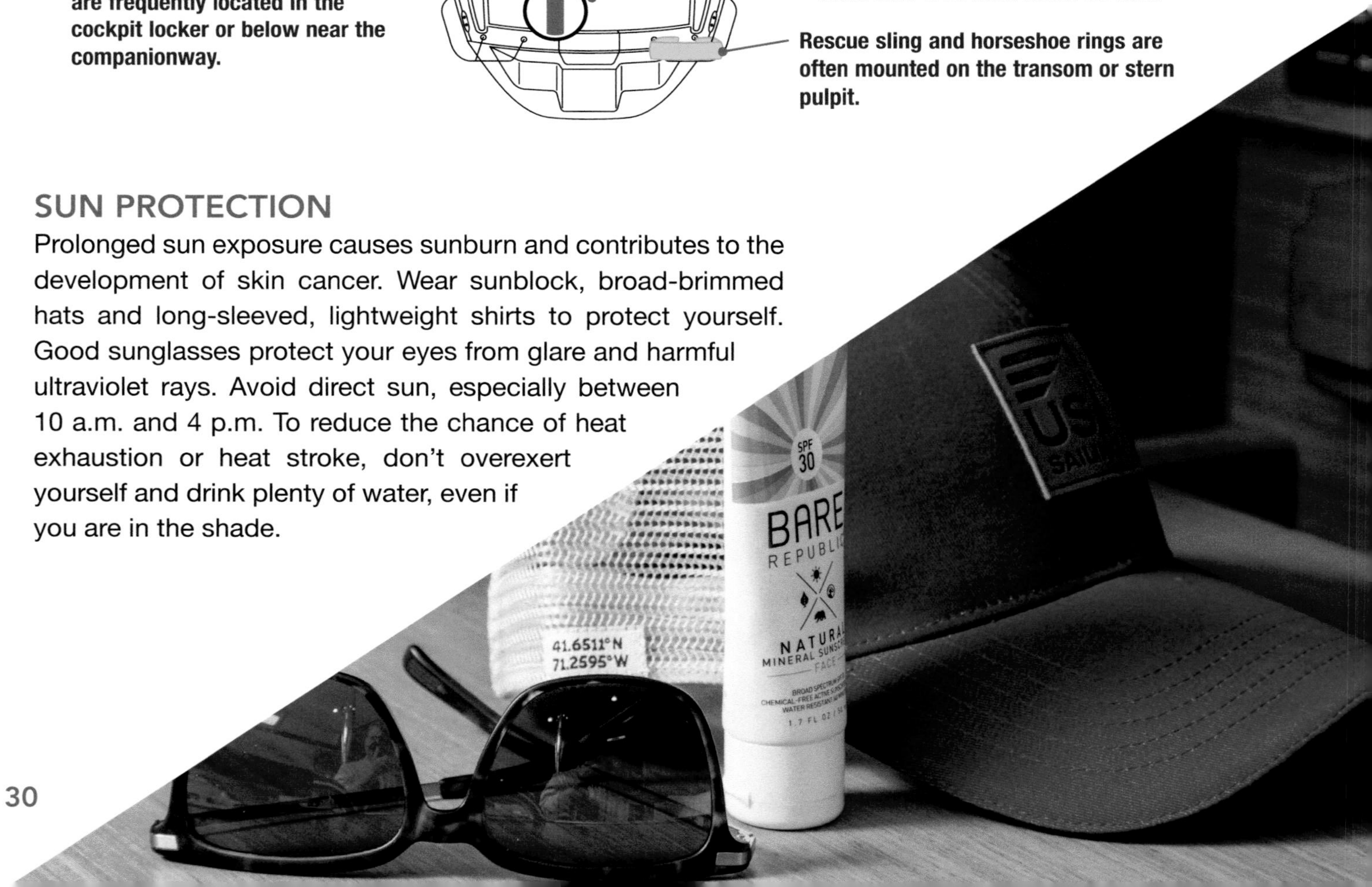

# LIFE JACKETS

Charter boats come equipped with life jackets to meet local requirements. Find and inspect the life jackets during the charter boat orientation. There should be one for each person on board, plus one throwable. Make sure they are in good condition, with no rips, tears, damaged straps, or illegible labeling. Put them on and adjust for a snug fit so they can't come off in the water. Stow them so they are readily available and not buried underneath the other items in the locker.

The life jackets provided may be intended for use when abandoning the boat and not be convenient for general wear. If you want specific features or if anyone intends to wear a life jacket much of the time, plan to bring your own. Charter boats may not provide life jackets in children's sizes. Correct sizing is important for small children. In some places, there are specific requirements for children of certain ages to wear life jackets. Check with the charter company and be prepared to bring your own.

If you decide to bring your own life jackets, fit and comfort are the most important factors to consider. You should also take into account the situation you will be sailing in relative to how much buoyancy the jacket provides, what color it is, the water temperature, and how much clothing, particularly foul weather gear, you may be wearing.

Complete the inspection and maintenance required by inflatable life jackets before leaving home, as the cylinders may not be available at your destination. Airline regulations regarding $CO_2$ cylinder transportation vary. Check with your carrier and the Transportation Security Administration (TSA).

Crew members should be encouraged to wear a life jacket any time they would be more comfortable doing so. The skipper will decide when life jackets are required for everyone based on whether you are sailing during the day or at night, inshore or offshore, and the wind and sea conditions. Life jackets should be considered when a crew member is alone on deck, when going forward, or during any emergency.

While often disregarded, some countries, including the United States, require life jackets to be carried when you are using the boat's dinghy.

It is good practice for children to wear a life jacket. In many areas it is required by law.

Life jackets provided may not be comfortable for extended wear. Consider bringing your own.

# COMMUNICATIONS

## MARINE VHF-FM RADIOS

The marine VHF-FM radio is the standard method of communication between vessels or between vessels and shore stations such as harbor masters and bridge attendants. Plan on line-of-sight transmission; the transmitting antenna must 'see' the receiving antenna, although sometimes greater range is possible. The Coast Guard typically sites their antennas on high points close to the shore to increase their range. An antenna atop a 50-foot mast would have a range of approximately eight miles, while one on a 1000-foot-high shore-side hill might reach 35 miles offshore.

## RADIO EMERGENCY CALL

1 Speak slowly and clearly.

2 Make the call on Channel 16. If the emergency is life-threatening, say **"Mayday, Mayday, Mayday."** If the call is urgent, but not life-threatening, use **"Pan-Pan, Pan-Pan, Pan-Pan."** If the call is a warning, use **"Sécurité, Sécurité, Sécurité."**

3 Identify the boat with call sign and/or name three times.

4 Give your location in either latitude and longitude or bearing and distance from a known object.

5 Give the number of people aboard and their status.

6 Specify the nature of the emergency.

7 Describe boat damage, if any, and seaworthiness.

8 End transmission with call sign and/or name and "over," which indicates you expect a response, or "out," which indicates you are finished.

9 Stay calm, stand by and listen for reply.

## CELL PHONES

While cell phones continue to make inroads and charter companies often provide a cell phone number for their service department, their usefulness is dependent on your plan and your carrier's service area. It can be useful to buy an inexpensive phone if yours does not have service where you are sailing. Cell phones do not have Digital Selective Calling (DSC) capabilities, nor can the Coast Guard use your cell signal to locate you.

## MARITIME MOBILE SERVICE IDENTITY (MMSI)

DSC requires that the radio be equipped with an MMSI number that identifies your boat (think of it like a phone number). MMSI numbers are issued by the Federal Communications Commission for vessels intending to cross (or communicate across) international borders (including Canada and Mexico). For vessels that operate solely within the United States, an MMSI number can be obtained from BoatUS.

# DIGITAL SELECTIVE CALLING (DSC)

Since 1999, all fixed-mount marine VHF-FM radios come with DSC capability built in, and it is an option with many hand-held units. DSC-enabled radios remain completely compatible with all non-DSC radios. However, a DSC radio can transmit information digitally as well as vocally, it can be used to call another DSC radio without using Channel 16, and it can send a digital distress message to the Coast Guard and any other DSC radio. If the radio is also GPS-enabled, the vessel's latitude/longitude position will be included in the distress message. GPS enabling also allows other DSC-equipped stations or boats to monitor your position.

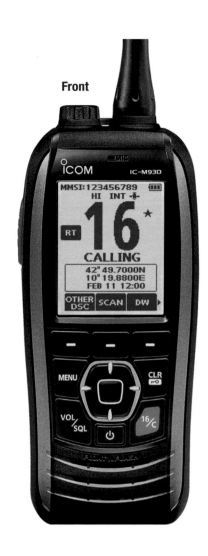

Front

## DSC-VHF radios will

▶ have one-button emergency transmit capability that sends out the vessel's unique MMSI number and, if properly connected to a GPS, the vessel's latitude/longitude.

▶ continue sending the distress signal even if the radio operator is incapacitated, but it has to be activated first.

▶ allow for an inexperienced VHF user to send, with the pressing of the one-button, a goof-proof continuous distress message.

▶ privately hail another DSC-equipped vessel or shore station with a known MMSI number. Similar to a telephone, it rings your radio notifying that you have a call. It will then automatically switch to the channel as that of your caller.

▶ transmit your vessel's position in digital format through the polling feature if properly connected to a GPS. This can be monitored by a DSC-equipped home station/fleet station or boat.

▶ work with non-DSC-equipped VHF radios.

## DSC-VHF radios will not

▶ be monitored by the U.S. Coast Guard in all areas until that area's Rescue 21 system is operational. However, DSC-equipped vessels in the area may receive your distress call.

▶ provide private radio-to-radio voice communication. After the private digital hail, DSC radios automatically switch to an open VHF channel for voice communications. Voice communication is carried on an active working channel chosen by the caller making the initial hail.

Back

**NOTE:** Distress button may be located on front, back, or side of your hand-held radio.

# SAIL INVENTORY

The vast majority of charter boats are sloops and your sail selection will be, in most cases, limited to main and jib. Some mains may have full-length battens which make the sail easier to control and reduce harmful flogging. While you may have a larger jib for light winds and a smaller one for heavier winds, most charter boats now come equipped with roller furling jibs. They can be adjusted in size by rolling them on the luff. Likewise, you may encounter a vertical batten or battenless mainsail that rolls into the mast. Both of these convenient systems require correct handling. Make sure the charter company instructs you on their proper use.

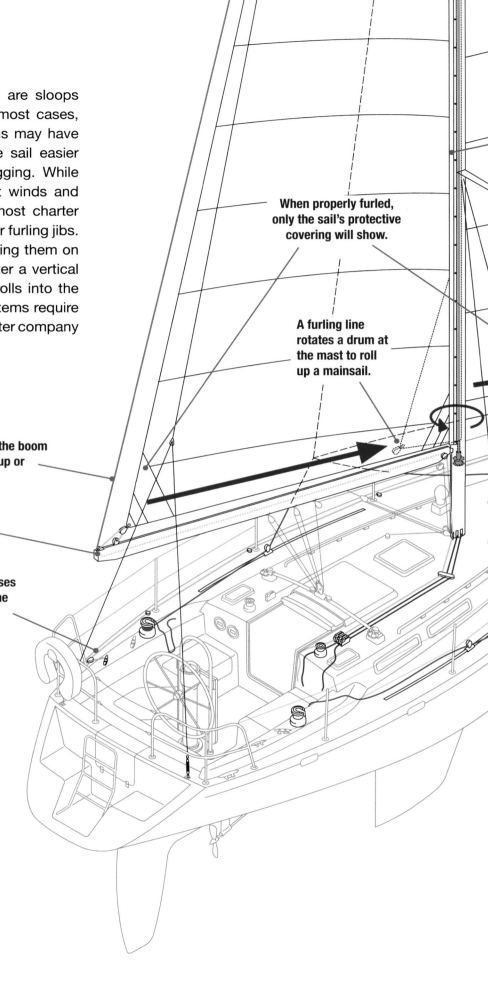

When properly furled, only the sail's protective covering will show.

A furling line rotates a drum at the mast to roll up a mainsail.

The topping lift supports the boom when reefing and rolling up or lowering the mainsail.

An extra long outhaul unrolls a roller furling mainsail.

The speed at which a sail unrolls increases rapidly as it is exposed to the wind. Some tension on the furling line controls how rapidly it unrolls and prevents overrides on the furling drum.

## Dos and Don'ts

▶ Do check the sail inventory and its condition during charter checkout.

▶ Do reef just before you need to, not just after.

▶ Do allow the wind to hold the mainsail slightly off the centerline when furling so it lines up with the mast slot.

▶ Do blanket the jib behind the main (if possible) when furling it.

▶ Don't force a sail to furl. Instead, find out what is stopping it.

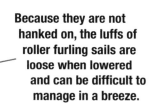

Because they are not hanked on, the luffs of roller furling sails are loose when lowered and can be difficult to manage in a breeze.

The furling drum turns to adjust the size of the jib and is controlled from the cockpit with a furling line.

# REDUCING SAIL AREA

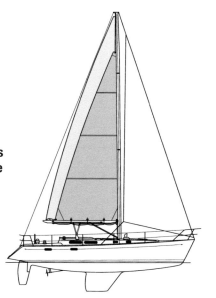

## REDUCE MAINSAIL FOR MORE CONTROL
Reducing the mainsail by reefing keeps the boat more upright and comfortable in heavy winds.

## REDUCE SAIL BY FURLING THE JIB
The roller furling jib can be fully extended for light winds and reduced as wind strength builds. Ask your charter company about the amount of sail to furl for different wind conditions.

### ROLLER FURLING MAINSAILS

**In-mast:** Unroll the main by pulling the outhaul while easing the furling line. Furl or reef by pulling the furling line while easing the outhaul. A bit of tension on the outhaul as you ease it will avoid wrinkles which can jam in the mast opening. A jam high up the mast can be very difficult to clear.

**In-boom:** Level the boom when furling or unfurling the main. Ease the furling line and hoist the main with the halyard. Lower or reef the sail by pulling the furling line while easing the halyard. Slight tension on the halyard helps the main roll up smoothly.

Marks and/or reinforcing patches indicating proper reefing positions are often added to the edge of the sail.

## DIFFERENT JIBS FOR DIFFERENT WINDS
The genoa ❶ overlaps the mast and provides more power in light winds. The jib ❷ keeps the boat from being overpowered in heavier winds.

# BIMINI TOPS

A bimini top (sun awning) is designed to be used while underway. Many have windows that allow you to see the sails while steering.

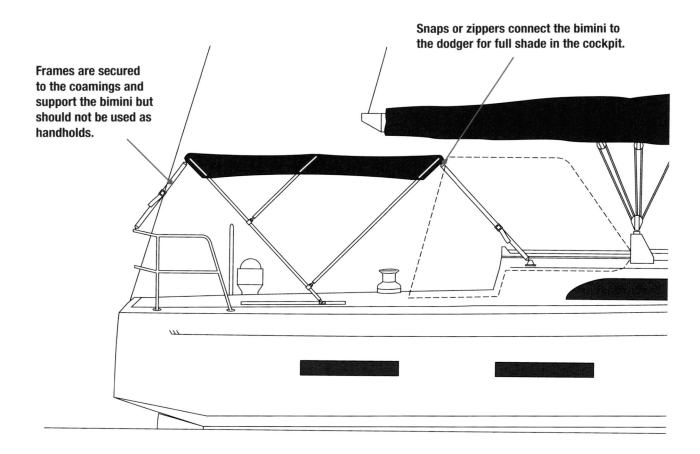

**Snaps or zippers connect the bimini to the dodger for full shade in the cockpit.**

**Frames are secured to the coamings and support the bimini but should not be used as handholds.**

# DODGERS

The dodger protects the front of the cockpit and companionway from spray. Plastic windows will provide visibility so you can see traffic, obstacles and sail trim.

You can snap on or zipper covers over the windows for privacy or protection from UV rays when you are not underway.

Use the handles on the side of the dodger as you move around the dodger.

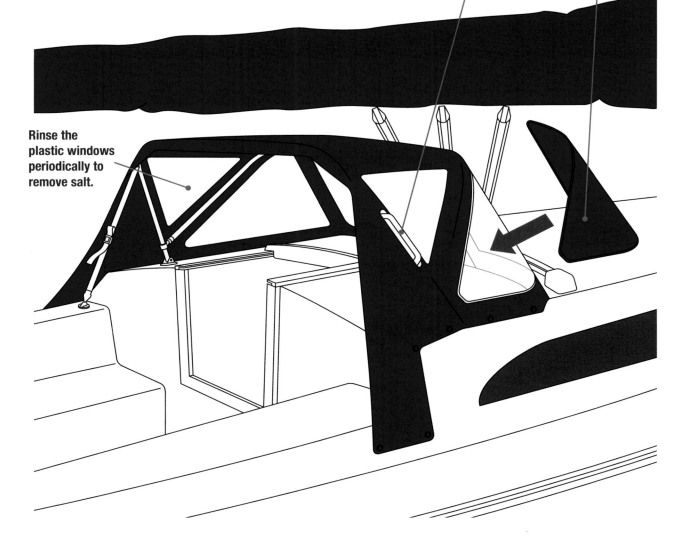

Rinse the plastic windows periodically to remove salt.

# Chapter 3

# **Cruising Skills**

It's a wise skipper who realizes that the finest passages are uneventful. We departed, we sailed, we arrived, and nothing happened. In order to ensure an 'uneventful passage' a skipper needs to master many skills, including docking and departing, close-quarters maneuvering under power, sail selection and helm balancing, anchoring, reefing, weather awareness and storm management, mooring pickups, Mediterranean mooring, international border crossings, and dealing with bridges and locks.

## WEATHER AND THE SAILING ENVIRONMENT

Before leaving the charter dock, check the weather forecast for the next few days. Local weather stations will carry up-to-date information. Rapid and/or large barometric pressure movements usually indicate major changes in the weather.

When warm, moist air cools below its dew point, fog forms. Bays and harbors can be shrouded in fog when cool water meets land-warmed air or a cold upwelling of water meets warm air as on the Northern California coast. When cold air meets a warm current, such as the Gulf Stream, fog forms at sea.

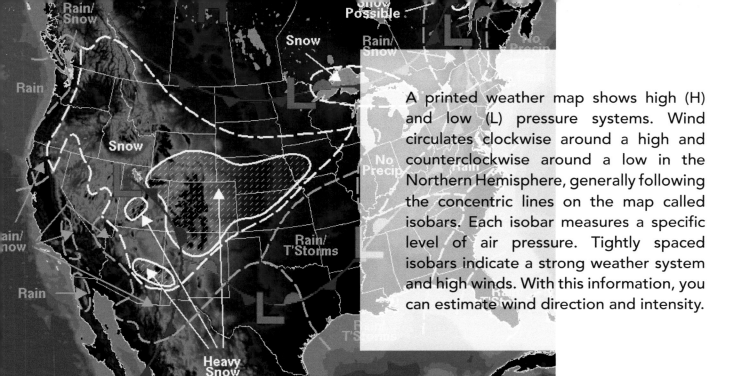

A printed weather map shows high (H) and low (L) pressure systems. Wind circulates clockwise around a high and counterclockwise around a low in the Northern Hemisphere, generally following the concentric lines on the map called isobars. Each isobar measures a specific level of air pressure. Tightly spaced isobars indicate a strong weather system and high winds. With this information, you can estimate wind direction and intensity.

## COLD FRONT ▼ ▼ ▼ ▼

Cold air replaces warm air, it moves rapidly, and is often accompanied by cumulus (or cumulonimbus) clouds. Heavy rain, strong winds and thunderstorms can occur. In the Northern Hemisphere, the wind veers (shifts clockwise) as the front passes.

## STATIONARY FRONT ⬭ ▼ ⬭ ▼

When air masses stall, the front doesn't move. Surface winds parallel the front. Weather associated with a stationary front is similar to a warm front but less intense.

## WARM FRONT ⬤ ⬤ ⬤ ⬤

Warm air replaces cold air, it moves slower (about half the speed of a cold front), and is generally accompanied by low-level stratus or altostratus clouds and showery conditions. If the air is unstable, there may be thundershowers and strong winds. In the Northern Hemisphere, the wind backs (shifts counterclockwise) as the front passes.

## RADIO WEATHER REPORTS

Local weather reports for U.S. coastal waters, updated every three hours, are usually available on VHF radio weather channels.

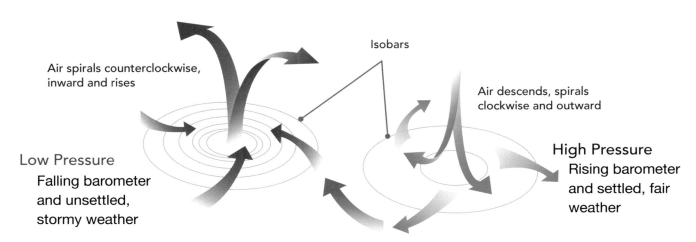

Isobars

Air spirals counterclockwise, inward and rises

Air descends, spirals clockwise and outward

Low Pressure
Falling barometer and unsettled, stormy weather

High Pressure
Rising barometer and settled, fair weather

## EAST COAST

East Coast weather patterns change constantly as the continental land mass reconfigures passing weather fronts. Cool Canadian highs mix with warm, moist air from the south to create towering cumulus clouds (photo left) that can become thunderstorms in the warmer months. Cold fronts move unpredictably but are usually followed by puffy and shifty northwesterlies. Early summer fog is common along New England's shores, particularly in the warm days of May and June.

## WEST COAST

West Coast weather forms over the Pacific Ocean. Winter storms track across the ocean and bring rain. From April through October a huge, relatively stationary offshore high pressure system, called the Pacific High, provides sunny weather and steady westerly breezes. Coastal areas experience regular sea breezes as the land heats up and the air flows from the sea to the land. Those areas adjacent to warm inland valleys frequently experience very strong afternoon winds and fog during the summer. Strong westerlies sometimes counter tidal currents and create unusually short and choppy waves such as those found on San Francisco Bay. Winter cold fronts over the desert cause strong easterlies, called Santa Anas, that can extend many miles offshore in Southern California.

## ISLAND WEATHER

In the tropics, where large land masses are scarce, trade winds predominate. Usually lighter in the morning, these winds peak at around 20 knots in the evening. Puffy, flat-bottomed clouds scud across the brilliant blue sky. Close to the equator, the Intertropical Convergence Zone (ITCZ) features light winds, squalls, and warm, overcast weather. The Caribbean's easterly Christmas winds may bring some wind velocities up to 30 knots. Spring features lighter breezes and dry weather.

## HURRICANE SEASONS

| Location | Months |
|---|---|
| Caribbean/East Coast | June - November |
| South Pacific | December - April |
| West Coast | June - November |

Rapidly moving black clouds indicate squalls. The clouds appear to be in long rows or lines. Squalls, usually of short duration, may have rain, strong winds and a change in wind direction; be prepared to respond quickly.

High cirrus clouds (mares' tails) usually indicate an approaching warm front with rain and wind changes in the next 48 hours. The cloud cover will become lower and denser.

# LEAVING THE DOCK

If you have a difficult time pushing a larger boat away from the dock, use the boat's spring lines for leverage. Plan your departure beforehand and make sure everyone on board knows what to expect and what to do. Crew should be prepared with fenders in hand to fend off obstacles or other boats as necessary. Go slowly and if things are not working, stop and start over.

## Dos and Don'ts

▶ Don't leave the dock without snugging the dinghy to the outboard (outside) aft quarter. Once in clear water, the dinghy can be towed off the stern.

▶ Do rig the spring lines at either the bow or stern, not amidships, when using them to swing the boat away from the dock.

▶ Do cast off dock lines in order of least tensioned first and the doubled-up working spring line last.

▶ Do account for the effect of prop walk on the boat's movement.

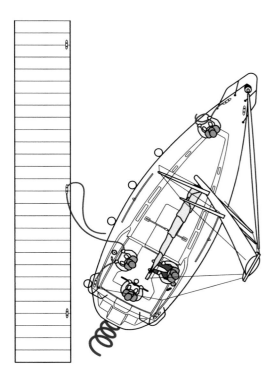

Doubling the spring line allows you to release it from aboard the boat. Pass it around the dock cleat and back to the boat. Bring the line in quickly to prevent fouling the propeller. Be prepared to cast the spring line completely off the boat should it snag on the dock.

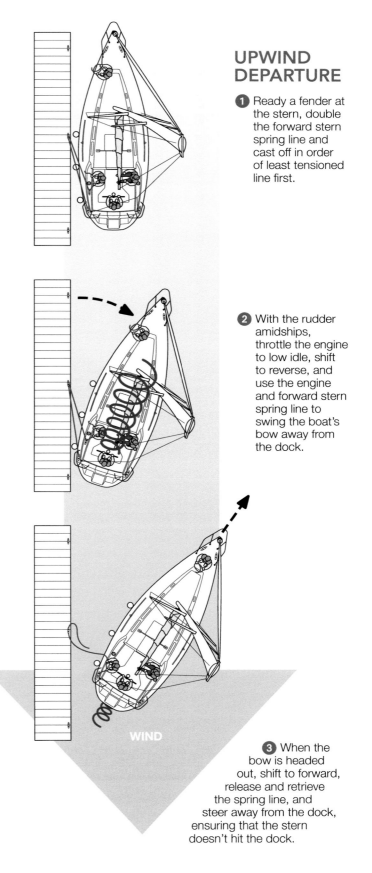

## UPWIND DEPARTURE

**1** Ready a fender at the stern, double the forward stern spring line and cast off in order of least tensioned line first.

**2** With the rudder amidships, throttle the engine to low idle, shift to reverse, and use the engine and forward stern spring line to swing the boat's bow away from the dock.

WIND

**3** When the bow is headed out, shift to forward, release and retrieve the spring line, and steer away from the dock, ensuring that the stern doesn't hit the dock.

## DOWNWIND DEPARTURE

## CROSSWIND DEPARTURE

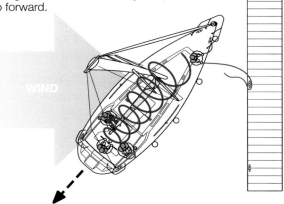

**3** Shift to reverse and use enough power to back away from the dock until upwind and clear of obstructions. Release and retrieve the spring line. Continue backing away until free to go forward.

WIND

**3** Shift to reverse, release and retrieve the spring line, and steer away from the dock, avoiding pilings and other obstructions on the dock. Continue in reverse until there is room to either turn the boat or go forward.

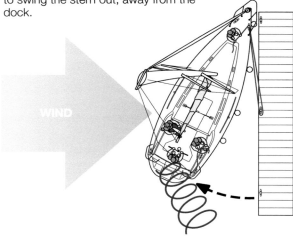

**2** Throttle the engine down to low idle. Shift to forward and motor slowly against the spring line. Gradually turn the rudder toward the dock to swing the stern out, away from the dock.

**2** Throttle the engine down to low idle. Shift to forward and motor slowly against the spring line. Gradually turn the rudder toward the dock to swing the stern out, away from the dock.

**1** Ready a fender near the bow, double the aft bow spring line, and cast off in order of least tensioned line first.

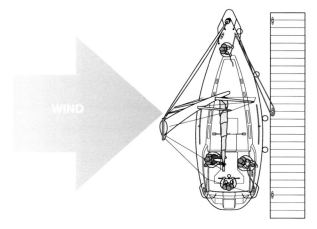

**1** Ready a fender near the bow, double the aft bow spring line, and cast off in order of least tensioned line first.

# MANEUVERING UNDER POWER

A boat's windage varies with the size and shape of the topsides. Windage increases with more wind and as the wind moves to the beam. Learn how windage influences the boat and practice compensating for it. Under power, you will feel the effects of windage increase as you slow down and the boat becomes more difficult to maneuver.

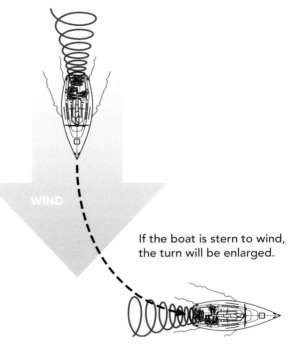

If the boat is head to wind, the wind's pressure on the bow causes the turn to be tighter.

If the boat is stern to wind, the turn will be enlarged.

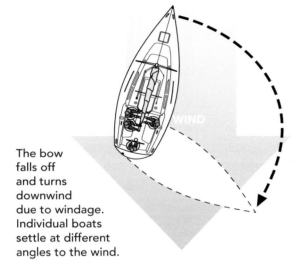

The bow falls off and turns downwind due to windage. Individual boats settle at different angles to the wind.

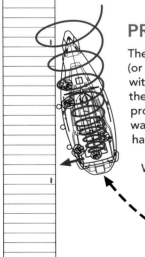

## PROP WALK

The propeller's rotation causes the stern to move sideways (or "walk"). In forward, this prop walk is easily corrected with the rudder because the "prop wash" (or water flow off the propeller) is directed across the rudder. In reverse, the prop wash is directed forward, not across the rudder. Prop walk cannot be corrected until the boat is moving aft and has sufficient water flow across the rudder.

While tied to the dock, check the direction of the prop walk by running the engine in reverse to see which way the prop wash flows. More boats back to port than starboard and knowing the direction in which your boat will walk can be very useful when maneuvering in tight quarters.

## STOPPING AND SHIFTING

▶ Shift gears only at idle.
▶ Shift into reverse to slow the forward motion of the boat. Too much throttle will induce prop walk and turn the boat.
▶ Windage changes the distance required for stopping.

## MAKING A TIGHT TURN

Turning in tight spaces, such as between moored boats or in a narrow marina fairway, requires a technique called "backing and filling." Prop walk becomes an asset in these situations. If your boat backs to port, you'll back and fill by turning the boat clockwise (bow to starboard). If it backs to starboard, make the turn counterclockwise. Boats will handle differently due to differences in underwater profile, propeller position, displacement and windage.

### Dos and Don'ts

▶ Do test forward and reverse gears of the transmission before you need them.

▶ Do check out the handling characteristics of your boat before entering close quarters.

▶ Do use the prop walk to help turn the boat.

▶ Don't forget that water must be flowing past the rudder for it to have any effect. The effect is greater in forward gear than in reverse.

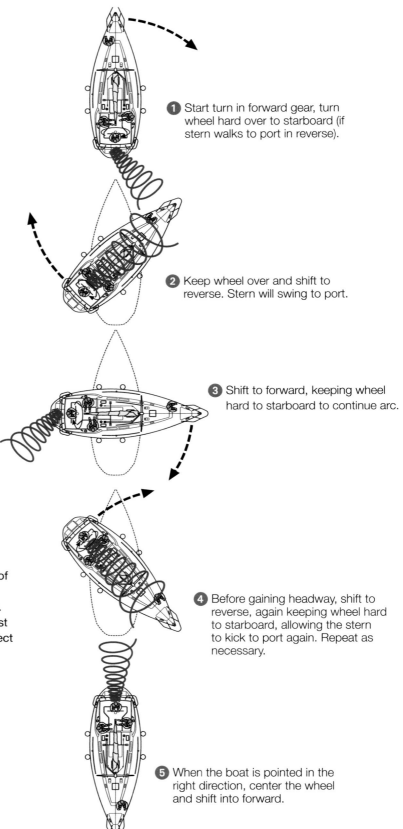

**1** Start turn in forward gear, turn wheel hard over to starboard (if stern walks to port in reverse).

**2** Keep wheel over and shift to reverse. Stern will swing to port.

**3** Shift to forward, keeping wheel hard to starboard to continue arc.

**4** Before gaining headway, shift to reverse, again keeping wheel hard to starboard, allowing the stern to kick to port again. Repeat as necessary.

**5** When the boat is pointed in the right direction, center the wheel and shift into forward.

# DOCKING

Docking a larger boat requires the same skills you learned on small boats. In addition, you may use midship spring lines for more control and you have to pay more attention to the boat's inertia and windage. If you have a choice, approach the dock with the bow into the wind to help slow your forward momentum. Use prop walk to bring the stern alongside the dock whenever possible.

## UPWIND DOCKING

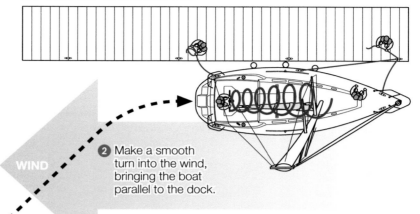

**WIND**

**2** Make a smooth turn into the wind, bringing the boat parallel to the dock.

**3** Put the engine into reverse to stop the boat. Secure the forward midship spring line, then the bow line and the other lines.

**1** Approach at approximately a 45 degree angle with enough power to keep steerageway.

### DOCKING CHECKLIST

▶ Check that all lines are clear of the propeller, including the dinghy painter.
▶ Secure the dinghy on the outboard quarter.
▶ Place fenders at dock level and fasten them to the stanchions' bases with a round turn and two half-hitches.

## DOWNWIND DOCKING

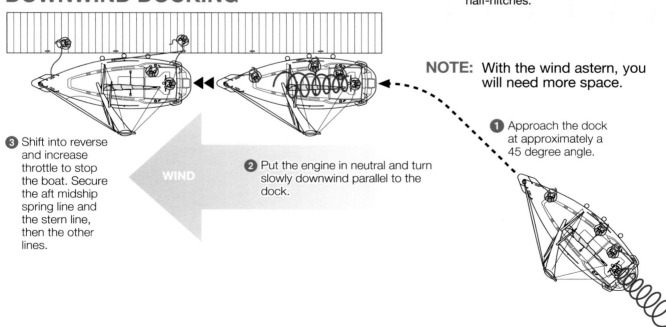

**3** Shift into reverse and increase throttle to stop the boat. Secure the aft midship spring line and the stern line, then the other lines.

**WIND**

**2** Put the engine in neutral and turn slowly downwind parallel to the dock.

**NOTE:** With the wind astern, you will need more space.

**1** Approach the dock at approximately a 45 degree angle.

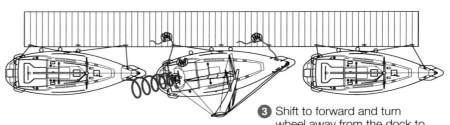

## CLOSE QUARTERS DOCKING

Motor slowly past your desired location to check the wind, current, and the direction of approach. Return with lines and fenders prepared. If you don't like the space situation or it exceeds your comfort zone, ask the dockmaster for another location.

**2** Come alongside the dock at a shallow angle and shift the engine into reverse to stop the boat and swing stern to the dock. Secure aft midship spring line.

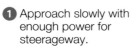

**1** Approach slowly with enough power for steerageway.

**3** Shift to forward and turn wheel away from the dock to bring the boat alongside the dock and hold it in position while the other lines are made fast.

## CROSSWIND DOCKING (LEEWARD SIDE)

**2** Make a tight turn to bring the boat parallel to the dock.

**3** Put the engine in reverse to stop. Secure the aft midship spring line. Shift to forward and turn the wheel so the rudder moves away from the dock. This will hold the boat against the dock until all lines are secured.

WIND

### Dos and Don'ts

▶ Do step onto the dock from the shrouds with dock lines in hand.

▶ Don't be afraid to abandon a docking that is not working and try again.

▶ Do use midship spring lines to bring the boat alongside the dock and hold it in position.

**1** At low speed, turn the boat directly into the wind until you are about a half boat length from the dock.

# CROSSWIND DOCKING (WINDWARD SIDE)

Approaching the windward side of the dock, the boat's windage will push you against the dock.

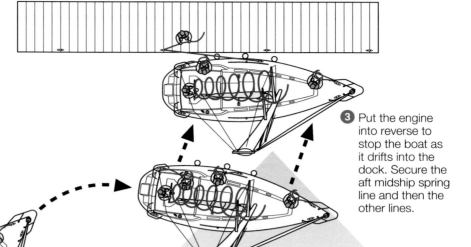

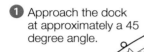

**1** Approach the dock at approximately a 45 degree angle.

**2** When half a boat length away, turn the boat almost parallel to the dock but with the bow cocked toward the wind.

**3** Put the engine into reverse to stop the boat as it drifts into the dock. Secure the aft midship spring line and then the other lines.

WIND

## SECURING THE BOAT

Led from midships, the aft spring line prevents forward motion and the forward spring line prevents motion aft. When securing the boat to a fixed dock in tidal waters, allow for the water level's rise and fall by leading the stern line to the outboard quarter.

Having secured fenders and dock lines in hand, this crew stands by the shrouds ready to step onto the dock.

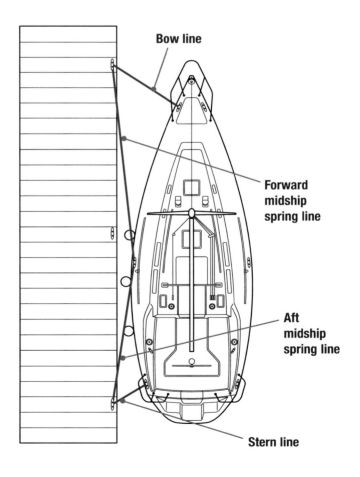

**Bow line**

**Forward midship spring line**

**Aft midship spring line**

**Stern line**

# MOTOR SAILING

There will be times when you may need or want to motor sail. Keep the sail properly trimmed to the apparent wind and avoid heading directly upwind. Flogging the main could cause damage for which a charter company can hold you responsible. Putting in a reef will flatten the sail and make trimming easier. Heeling may affect engine operation, so check your oil pressure and temperature gauges regularly.

**Except for boats less than 12 meters (39.4 feet) in length, the Navigation Rules require an inverted black cone to be displayed when motor sailing.**

## Dos and Don'ts

▶ Do trim your sails to the wind when motor sailing.
▶ Don't forget the apparent wind goes forward when your speed increases.
▶ Do keep the boat upright when motor sailing.
▶ Don't flog the mainsail by motor sailing directly into the wind.
▶ Do remember you are a powerboat under the Navigation Rules.

## When Moving Slowly

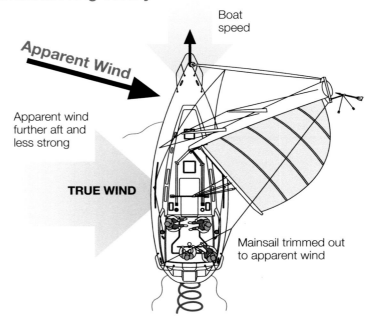

Boat speed

Apparent Wind

Apparent wind further aft and less strong

TRUE WIND

Mainsail trimmed out to apparent wind

**NOTE:** When motor sailing, especially in light winds, the forward motion will draw the apparent wind toward the bow. Keep your sails trimmed to the wind as indicated by the masthead fly or the telltales.

## When Moving Faster

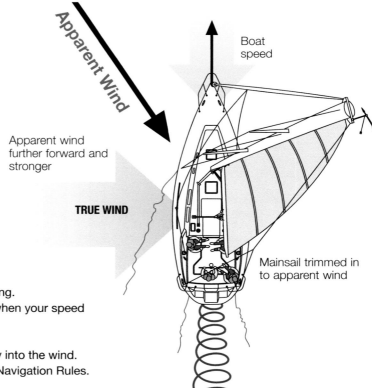

Boat speed

Apparent Wind

Apparent wind further forward and stronger

TRUE WIND

Mainsail trimmed in to apparent wind

# BIG BOAT CREWING

Crewing on a larger boat demands coordination and teamwork not only between the helm and the crew, but also among the crew themselves. Where brute strength might suffice on a smaller boat, you will need to focus instead on anticipation, timing and execution. Communication, especially in advance of maneuvers, is the cornerstone of success.

## HAND SIGNALS

Commonly agreed upon hand signals are useful in situations when it's hard to be heard over the wind or other noises. Here are some typical signals:

**When raising or lowering sail:** thumbs up means go higher; thumbs down means keep lowering; and clenched fist means stop.

**When trimming sails:** pointing in the direction of the sail means let it out; twirling your index finger means trim the sheet in; a clenched fist means stop.

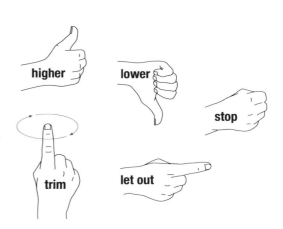

**Dos and Don'ts**

▶ Do have the helmsman hold the bow close to the wind to luff the jib after a tack so the crew can grind in the sail under reduced load.

▶ Do talk over sailing maneuvers beforehand so that everyone knows what is going to happen.

▶ Don't attempt maneuvers that require a greater skill level than you have.

▶ Do assign at least one crew member to always be responsible for looking under the jib to leeward for obstructions or other boats.

▶ Don't over tighten a line on an electric winch. Overrides can be especially problematic on these convenient devices.

▶ Don't ever leave winch handles in winches when not in use.

## ELECTRIC WINCHES

Electric winches are wonderful when there is 'heavy lifting' to be done. However, they are very powerful and need to be used with care and attention. If anything binds or catches (e.g., mainsail cars, battens in the lazy jacks, lines twisted in blocks or fairleads), the winch will attempt to overpower the jam, causing significant damage. Monitor your progress, watching for potential jams and listening for the tell-tale sound of the winch motor loading.

The activation button, finger or foot will usually have a partial or complete cap to prevent accidental activation.

**Dos and Don'ts**

▶ Do take a moment to make sure hair and fingers are clear of the winch.

▶ Do make sure you are braced in a way that will not cause you to accidentally activate the winch if the boat rocks.

▶ Do ensure the manual winch handle is removed.

▶ Do load the line onto the winch in a clockwise direction.

▶ Do manually pull all the slack out of the line to see AND feel that the line, when loaded, will run fairly.

▶ Do keep a very close eye on the working end of the line to make sure nothing gets fouled.

▶ Don't forget, once you have finished using the electric winch for the hard work, to close the safety cap on the activation button.

▶ Do remember that easing the line on an electric winch is the same as with a manual winch.

# DOWNWIND SAILING

When sailing long distances, comfort becomes important. If your destination is downwind, you might put your boat on a run, but you will roll and pitch in moderate sea conditions. The mainsail will blanket the jib, reducing the sail's pull and creating a hazard as the jib sheets swing back and forth across the foredeck. You also risk sailing by the lee and jibing the mainsail accidentally. By heading up to a broad reach, you will sail safer and more comfortably.

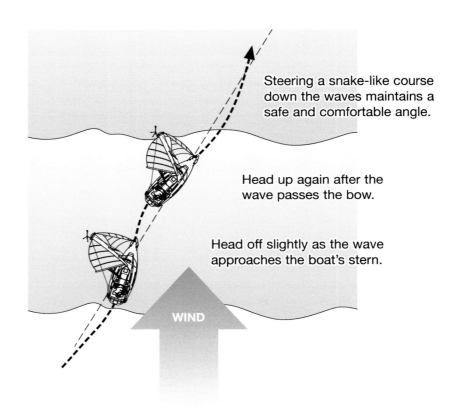

Steering a snake-like course down the waves maintains a safe and comfortable angle.

Head up again after the wave passes the bow.

Head off slightly as the wave approaches the boat's stern.

Running can cause uncomfortable rolling and pitching and accidental jibes.

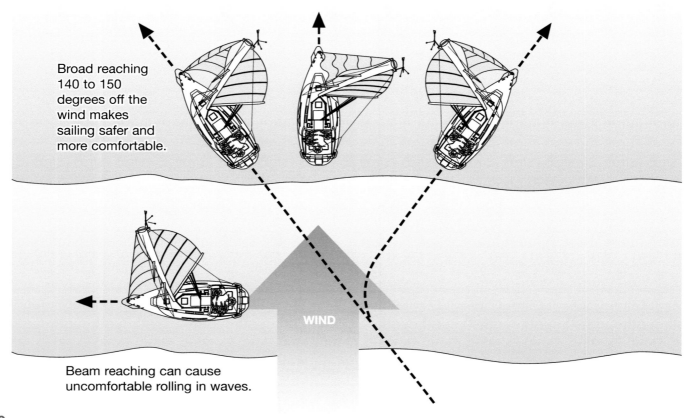

Broad reaching 140 to 150 degrees off the wind makes sailing safer and more comfortable.

Beam reaching can cause uncomfortable rolling in waves.

# HEAVING-TO

Heaving-to will stop the boat at a safe angle to the wind and the boat will maintain that position unattended. This allows the crew to deal with reefing, gear failure, injuries, or just eat lunch. When heaving-to the vessel is not entirely stopped. It is still underway and will be affected by wind, current, and wave action. Situational awareness is necessary to keep the boat away from land, shallows, or other obstacles to leeward. It is also subject to the Navigation Rules, including keeping a watch. There are some right-of-way advantages to heaving-to on starboard tack.

Ensure that you have the correct sail complement. If your jib is greater than 100%, roll it smaller so it doesn't chafe against the spreader tip. Start the maneuver by sailing close-hauled, with the jib sheeted in tightly so it is quite flat. Begin to tack slowly, without releasing the sheets. Stop the tack when the boat is head to wind, with the jib slightly backed and the main luffing. As the boat speed drops, continue to turn the wheel farther and farther to windward in order to hold the boat head to wind. When the boat comes to a complete stop and the rudder no longer works, the backed jib will complete the maneuver for you and the rudder will be in the correct position.

When you don't want to tack, you can grind the jib to windward using the windward sheet while slowly steering more and more upwind until the boat comes to a complete stop and begins to drift downwind.

Adjust the main and the wheel to reduce heel and fine-tune the angle at which the boat lies to the wind. Ideally the boat will be lying on a close reach, drifting downwind, and making little or no headway.

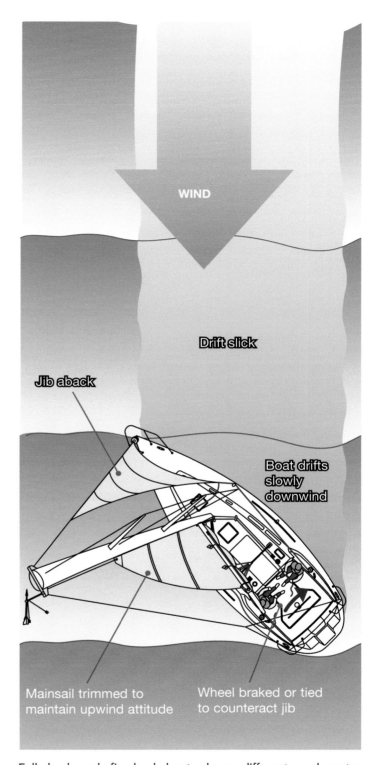

WIND

Drift slick

Jib aback

Boat drifts slowly downwind

Mainsail trimmed to maintain upwind attitude

Wheel braked or tied to counteract jib

Full keel and fin keel boats have different underwater configurations and may require different mainsail trim to remain hove-to. Experiment with your boat to discover what trim works best.

# DEPOWERING SAILS

As wind speed increases, steering becomes more difficult due to increasing weather helm and/or excessive heel. Depowering the sails will keep the boat more upright, more comfortable, and easier to control. When the procedures explained below are no longer sufficient, it is time to reef.

## FEATHER THE SAILS

When sailing upwind and a strong puff hits, you can steer the boat slightly into the No-Go Zone until the forward edge of the sails luff. This will reduce heeling and weather helm. As the puff passes, steer back on course and the boat will pick up speed again.

## DEPOWER THE MAINSAIL BY ADJUSTING ITS SHAPE

Tighten the outhaul to flatten the mainsail. Tension the luff of the mainsail to reposition the draft forward by tightening the cunningham (if equipped) or the halyard. Tighten the adjustable backstay (if equipped) to flatten the middle of the mainsail.

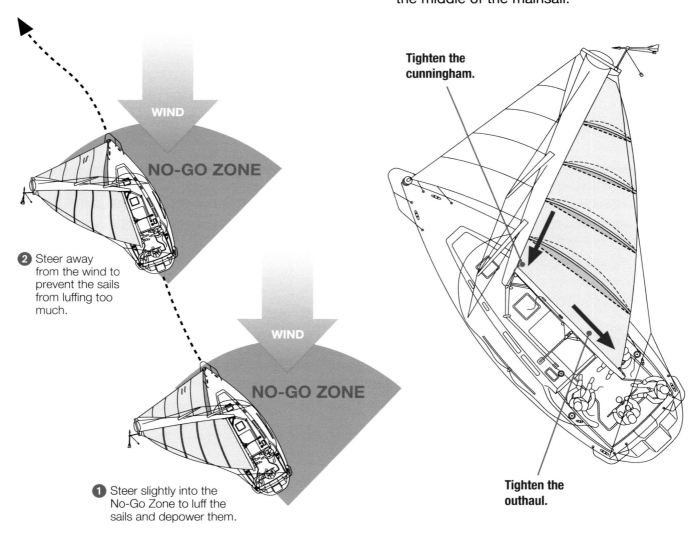

WIND

NO-GO ZONE

❷ Steer away from the wind to prevent the sails from luffing too much.

WIND

NO-GO ZONE

❶ Steer slightly into the No-Go Zone to luff the sails and depower them.

**Tighten the cunningham.**

**Tighten the outhaul.**

## DEPOWER THE MAINSAIL BY ADJUSTING ITS TRIM

Easing the traveler to leeward lessens the pressure on the entire sail.

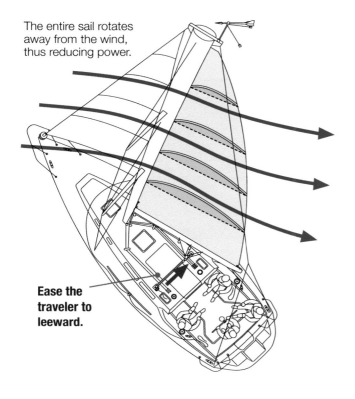

The entire sail rotates away from the wind, thus reducing power.

**Ease the traveler to leeward.**

## DEPOWER THE MAINSAIL BY ADJUSTING ITS TWIST

Ease the mainsheet and vang to allow the aft end of the boom to rise and the top of the mainsail to twist off to leeward. Move the traveler to windward to keep the lower portion of the mainsail properly trimmed.

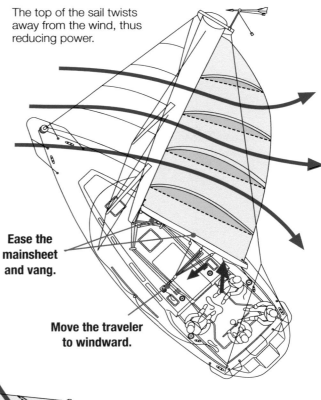

The top of the sail twists away from the wind, thus reducing power.

**Ease the mainsheet and vang.**

**Move the traveler to windward.**

## DEPOWER THE JIB BY ADJUSTING ITS SHAPE

Move the fairleads aft to flatten the foot of the jib and twist the top to leeward. Tension the luff of the jib to reposition the draft forward by tightening the adjustable backstay (if equipped) or the halyard.

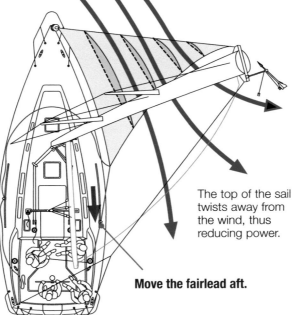

The top of the sail twists away from the wind, thus reducing power.

**Move the fairlead aft.**

### DEPOWERING CHECKLIST

- ▶ Feather the sails.
- ▶ Ease the mainsheet.
- ▶ Flatten the mainsail by tightening the outhaul.
- ▶ Tighten the cunningham and/or halyard.
- ▶ Ease the traveler to leeward.
- ▶ Tighten the backstay (if equipped).
- ▶ Move the jib fairleads aft.
- ▶ Reef the sails.

# REEFING

Reefing is just another sail adjustment. With the correct amount of sail area and proper sail trim, only small adjustments to the helm are needed. Increasing wind changes this wonderful boat/wind balance, resulting in undesirable increases in both heel and weather helm. Reefing (reducing sail area) will correct both and restore the balance. Partially rolling the headsail may be the place to start, reducing it to 90–95%, which will put the clew just forward of the shrouds. The headsail will be much easier to roll up if you bear away until it just enters the wind shadow of the mainsail (this is known as blanketing the jib). If further reductions in sail area are necessary, reef the mainsail, and roll the jib smaller.

It is safer (and easier) to reef before the boat is overpowered, so remember that the answer to the question "*I wonder if I should reef?*" is always YES!

## CHANGING HEADSAILS WITH HANK-ON SAILS

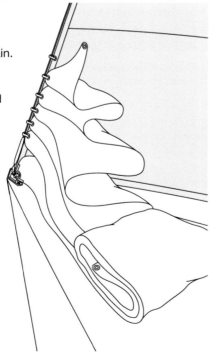

1 When possible, blanket the headsail with the main. Lower it, remove and secure the halyard and sheets, then unhank and stow the sail.

2 Adjust the jib fairleads and reeve the sheets (if necessary).

3 Bring the new jib on deck, tack it down and hank it on.

4 Attach the sheets and halyard and check that all lines have fairleads.

5 Hoist the jib, tension and cleat the halyard, then trim the sail.

With a roller furling jib, it's easy to shorten the sail by furling the jib on the headstay. Roll up the sail until you have a comfortable heeling angle. Check with the charter company if there is a preferred amount of sail to furl.

When reefing the jib, move the jib sheet fairleads forward to maintain proper sheeting angle.

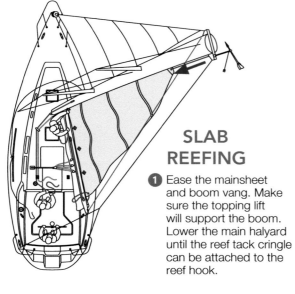

## SLAB REEFING

**1** Ease the mainsheet and boom vang. Make sure the topping lift will support the boom. Lower the main halyard until the reef tack cringle can be attached to the reef hook.

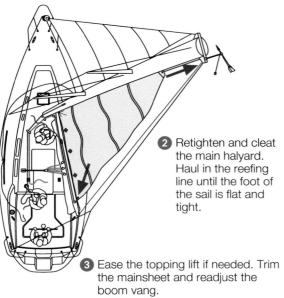

**2** Retighten and cleat the main halyard. Haul in the reefing line until the foot of the sail is flat and tight.

**3** Ease the topping lift if needed. Trim the mainsheet and readjust the boom vang.

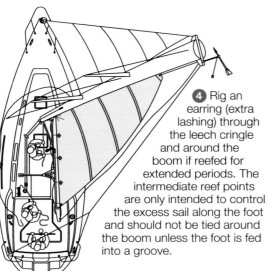

**4** Rig an earring (extra lashing) through the leech cringle and around the boom if reefed for extended periods. The intermediate reef points are only intended to control the excess sail along the foot and should not be tied around the boom unless the foot is fed into a groove.

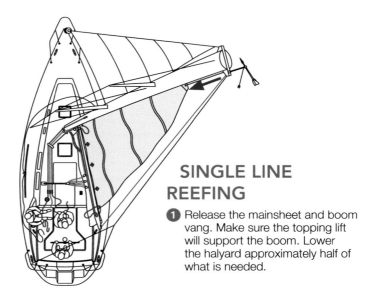

## SINGLE LINE REEFING

**1** Release the mainsheet and boom vang. Make sure the topping lift will support the boom. Lower the halyard approximately half of what is needed.

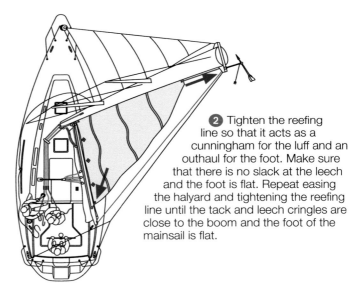

**2** Tighten the reefing line so that it acts as a cunningham for the luff and an outhaul for the foot. Make sure that there is no slack at the leech and the foot is flat. Repeat easing the halyard and tightening the reefing line until the tack and leech cringles are close to the boom and the foot of the mainsail is flat.

**3** Ease the topping lift if needed. Trim the mainsheet and readjust the boom vang.

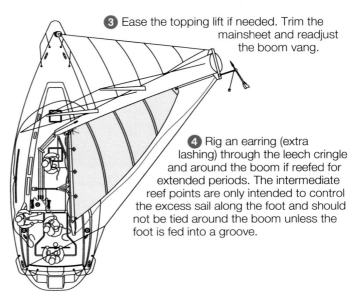

**4** Rig an earring (extra lashing) through the leech cringle and around the boom if reefed for extended periods. The intermediate reef points are only intended to control the excess sail along the foot and should not be tied around the boom unless the foot is fed into a groove.

# SQUALLS AND STORMS

Blackening and growing clouds, especially in the tropics, usually indicate short-term storms called squalls. If you are close to a harbor of refuge, a short motor sail to a protected area may be the best solution. If obstructions are close by or the only safe harbor is some distance to windward, sail toward deeper water. Prepare for the worst by reefing, changing to smaller sails or heaving-to with adequate sea room. Sailing off the wind reduces the strain on the boat.

Defined groups of dark clouds often bring squalls, which may include strong wind, heavy rain or both. Only infrequently do these pass without incident.

Roll the furling headsail tightly and wrap the jib sheets around the sail. Tension jib sheets and cleat them.

## HEAVY WEATHER PREPARATION

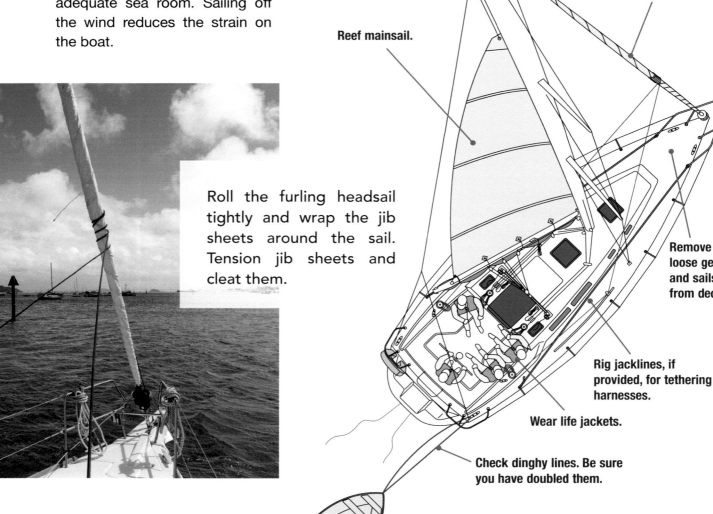

Reef mainsail.

Furl headsail tightly.

Remove all loose gear and sails from deck.

Rig jacklines, if provided, for tethering harnesses.

Wear life jackets.

Check dinghy lines. Be sure you have doubled them.

# ANCHORING

On a typical cruise you may anchor two or three times a day to take advantage of different opportunities. Master the techniques and skills of anchoring thoroughly so you can enjoy your cruising. Success depends on preparation, planning and practice. Learn how to handle the different scenarios.

## ANCHORING CHECKLIST

▶ Compare the anchorage with your chart.
▶ Determine the prevailing wind and current for the duration of your stay.
▶ Select your spot and brief the crew on your anchoring plan.
▶ Anchor in the same configuration as your neighbors so all boats swing alike.
▶ Secure the bitter end of your anchor rode before you lower the anchor.
▶ Calculate your rode length by adding your boat's freeboard to the tidal range and water depth and multiplying that figure by the desired ratio, usually 4:1 to 7:1.
▶ If the anchorage is not crowded, you will be most comfortable with a 7:1 ratio for a chain and line rode
▶ Typical scope for an all chain rode is 4:1.
▶ Boats will swing in smaller arcs when anchored with an all chain rode.
▶ Boats will swing in wider arcs when using rope rather than all chain rode.

## REID HARBOR

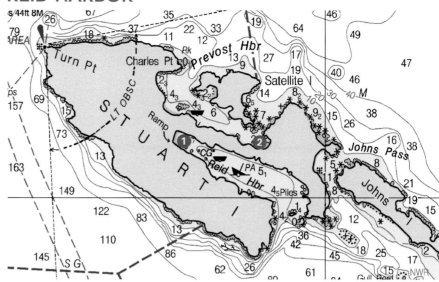

**1** While the entrance to Reid Harbor is narrow, the chart shows 4 fathoms, 2 feet (or 26 feet) of water in the center to the west of the two small islands. Anchor well into the harbor to the northwest of the Coast Guard buoy, where you are protected from everything except a strong southeasterly wind.

**2** This location will provide excellent protection from the southeast. Enter Prevost Harbor on the west side of Satellite Island; do not attempt the rock strewn pass on the east side of the island.

## HIDDEN HARBOR

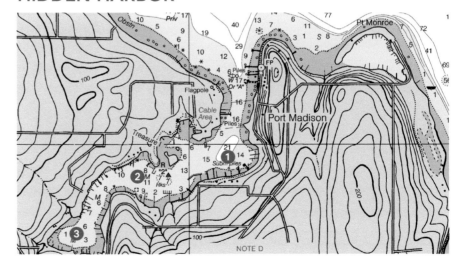

**1** This location is very well protected from all winds except from due north. Anchor far enough east to allow passage of through traffic.

**2** This location, while a little smaller, offers very good protection from

north winds. Don't anchor so that you block access to the docks along the north shore.

**3** This location is protected in all directions, but check for tidal changes during your intended stay.

# COMBINED EFFECTS OF WIND AND CURRENT

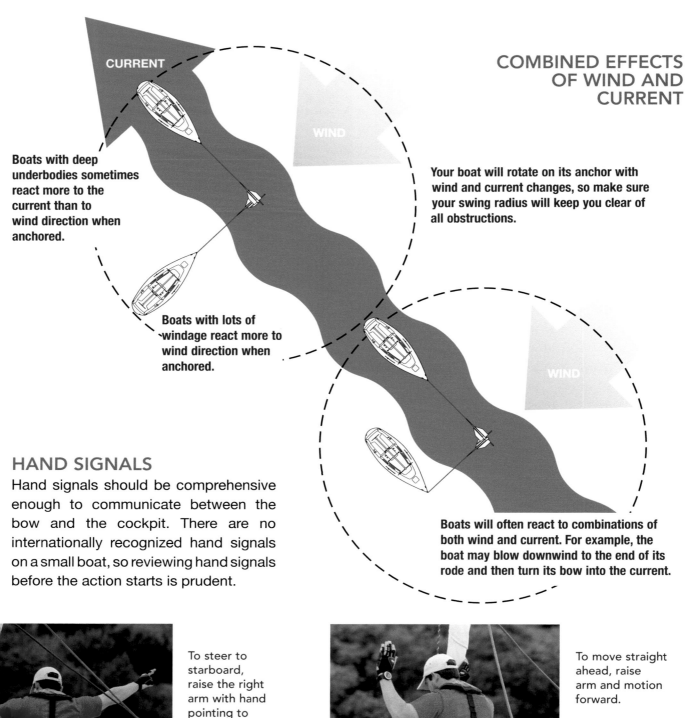

**CURRENT**

**WIND**

**WIND**

Boats with deep underbodies sometimes react more to the current than to wind direction when anchored.

Boats with lots of windage react more to wind direction when anchored.

Your boat will rotate on its anchor with wind and current changes, so make sure your swing radius will keep you clear of all obstructions.

Boats will often react to combinations of both wind and current. For example, the boat may blow downwind to the end of its rode and then turn its bow into the current.

## HAND SIGNALS

Hand signals should be comprehensive enough to communicate between the bow and the cockpit. There are no internationally recognized hand signals on a small boat, so reviewing hand signals before the action starts is prudent.

To steer to starboard, raise the right arm with hand pointing to starboard.

To move straight ahead, raise arm and motion forward.

To indicate stop, raise arm with closed fist.

To indicate reverse, raise arm with palm facing aft.

# ANCHORING UNDER POWER

As anchorages become more crowded, the age-old technique of anchoring under sail has become less common. While a skilled sailor can still derive much satisfaction from executing this maneuver under sail, the use of the engine provides more control and is now the norm. As with so many nautical maneuvers, the key to success is preparation.

**2** Stop the boat just upwind of where you have decided to place your anchor, with the wind slightly on the anchor side of the bow. If the anchor is on the centerline, then head to wind is fine. As the bow begins to blow downwind, quickly lower the anchor to the bottom and then deploy the rode at the same speed that the boat blows downwind. If there is no wind, then slowly motor in reverse. Prop walk may determine which way the boat turns.

**3** Continue deploying the rode as the boat blows downwind. Do not be alarmed by the fact that the boat settles to a broad reach, as this is normal.

**1** Approach the anchorage under power, with sails furled, ground tackle ready, and the crew briefed. When towing a dinghy, shorten the painter so that it cannot foul the propeller or tie it alongside.

**4** When sufficient rode has been deployed, cleat it. This should cause the boat to come head to wind again.

## Dos and Don'ts

▶ Do furl your sails before anchoring.

▶ Deal with your dinghy before anchoring.

▶ Don't drop the anchor and rode in a heap. Lower the anchor first and feed out the rode as the boat blows downwind.

▶ Do keep track of how much rode you let out.

▶ Do remember that arriving vessels must respect the rights of vessels already anchored.

**5** After waiting to give the anchor a chance to settle into the bottom, shift into reverse and **GRADUALLY** apply power. Check a range abeam to ensure that you have set the hook.

# MULTIPLE ANCHOR TECHNIQUES

There are conditions in which the use of two anchors is recommended. However, a change in wind direction can have you dependent on only one anchor. In the following scenarios below, each anchor must be of sufficient size and each rode long enough to hold the boat independently.

## TWO ANCHORS OFF THE BOW

When the wind is forecast to blow hard but not change direction, this method will increase holding power and reduce swing. An imaginary line between the two anchors should be perpendicular to the wind. The angle between the two anchor rodes should be approximately 60 degrees.

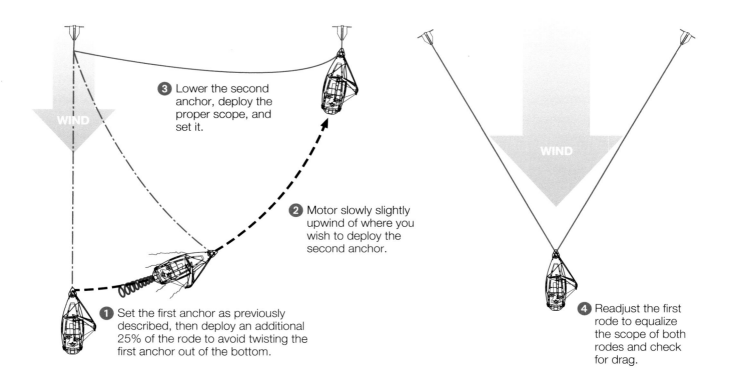

WIND

**3** Lower the second anchor, deploy the proper scope, and set it.

**2** Motor slowly slightly upwind of where you wish to deploy the second anchor.

**1** Set the first anchor as previously described, then deploy an additional 25% of the rode to avoid twisting the first anchor out of the bottom.

WIND

**4** Readjust the first rode to equalize the scope of both rodes and check for drag.

## SETTING A SECOND ANCHOR WITH THE DINGHY

You can use your dinghy to deploy a second anchor. This is most easily accomplished with two people in the dinghy. Secure the bitter end of the rode to your boat and load the anchor and all the rode into the dinghy. Row or motor away, deploying the rode as you go. This avoids having to drag the line through the water. As an alternative, you can put the anchor and only a few feet of the rode into the dinghy and deploy the rode as you row or motor away. Either method will be very difficult with an all chain rode.

Because the anchor will fall back towards the boat when you drop it, go a little farther from the boat than where you want the anchor to set. When you have reached the proper location, drop the anchor. Return to the boat and set the second anchor using the motor.

## BOW AND STERN ANCHORING

Where room to swing is limited, this method will hold the boat in place. Wind/current on the beam may cause the anchors to drag.

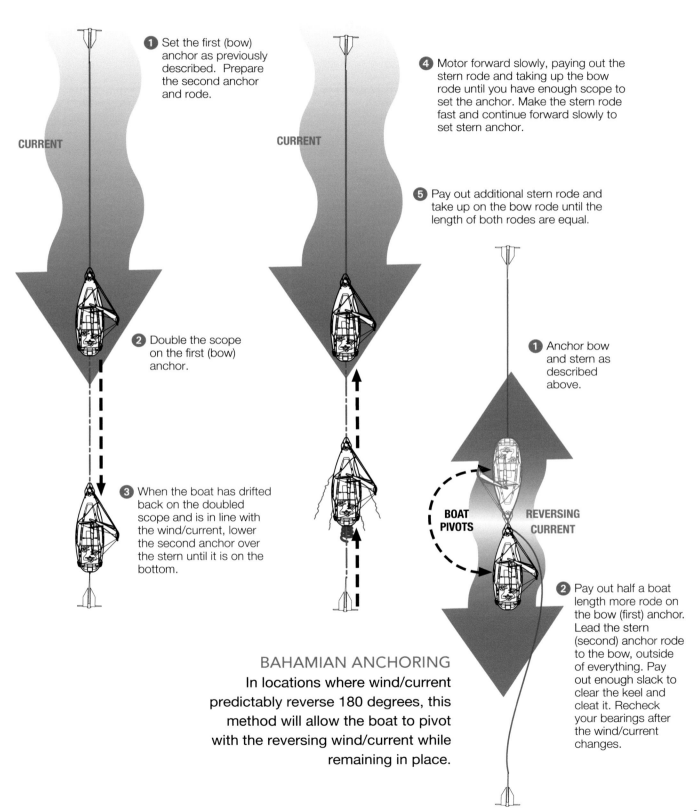

**CURRENT**

**1** Set the first (bow) anchor as previously described. Prepare the second anchor and rode.

**2** Double the scope on the first (bow) anchor.

**3** When the boat has drifted back on the doubled scope and is in line with the wind/current, lower the second anchor over the stern until it is on the bottom.

**CURRENT**

**4** Motor forward slowly, paying out the stern rode and taking up the bow rode until you have enough scope to set the anchor. Make the stern rode fast and continue forward slowly to set stern anchor.

**5** Pay out additional stern rode and take up on the bow rode until the length of both rodes are equal.

## BAHAMIAN ANCHORING

In locations where wind/current predictably reverse 180 degrees, this method will allow the boat to pivot with the reversing wind/current while remaining in place.

**BOAT PIVOTS**

**REVERSING CURRENT**

**1** Anchor bow and stern as described above.

**2** Pay out half a boat length more rode on the bow (first) anchor. Lead the stern (second) anchor rode to the bow, outside of everything. Pay out enough slack to clear the keel and cleat it. Recheck your bearings after the wind/current changes.

## SNUBBER

Because all chain rodes do not stretch, rig a snubber to absorb shock loads from strong wind gusts. Attach one end of a three-strand line to the chain with a devil's claw, a chain hook, or a rolling hitch and cleat the other to the boat. Now deploy more chain until the snubber takes the load. This also takes the load off the windlass and puts it on the cleat where it belongs.

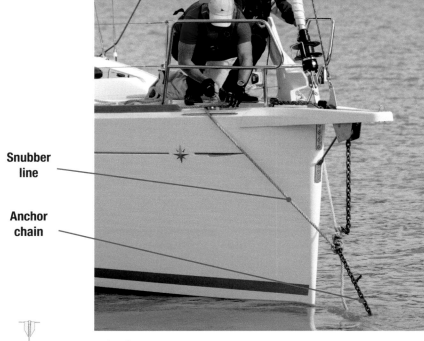

**Snubber line**

**Anchor chain**

## DRAGGING ANCHORS

Small changes in a range abeam may be caused by changes in wind, current and tide. Significant and continuing changes mean your anchor is dragging. Increasing your scope may solve the problem. If not, retrieve your anchor and reset it. If that doesn't stop the dragging, move to another location or use a different type of anchor.

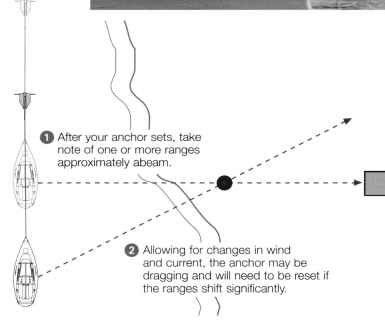

1 After your anchor sets, take note of one or more ranges approximately abeam.

2 Allowing for changes in wind and current, the anchor may be dragging and will need to be reset if the ranges shift significantly.

## RAISING AN ANCHOR UNDER POWER

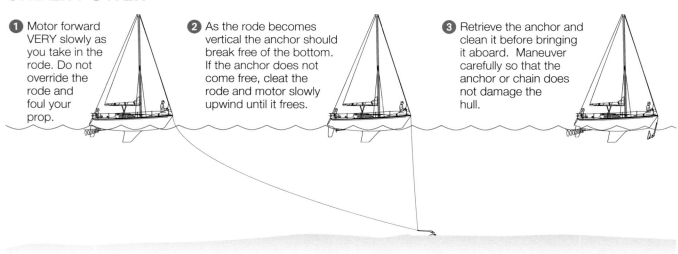

1 Motor forward VERY slowly as you take in the rode. Do not override the rode and foul your prop.

2 As the rode becomes vertical the anchor should break free of the bottom. If the anchor does not come free, cleat the rode and motor slowly upwind until it frees.

3 Retrieve the anchor and clean it before bringing it aboard. Maneuver carefully so that the anchor or chain does not damage the hull.

## UNFOULING ANCHORS

Shifting wind/current, a boat dragging its anchor, or a departure from a crowded Mediterranean mooring can cause rodes to foul (tangle). With a combination of patience, cooperation, and the careful placement of fenders, the rodes can be cleared.

If you find yourself lifting another boat's rode as you retrieve your anchor, first alert the other boat. Then support their rode with one of your dock lines. This will allow you to lower your anchor and work it free of the other rode.

## USING A TRIP LINE

If you anticipate difficulty recovering your anchor, rig a trip line when you deploy the anchor. The line should be a little longer than the depth of the water at the highest tide. One end is attached to the crown of the anchor and the other leads to a small float on the surface. Not only will this mark the location of your anchor, but it can be used to trip the anchor (pull it out of the bottom backwards) when normal retrieval doesn't work.

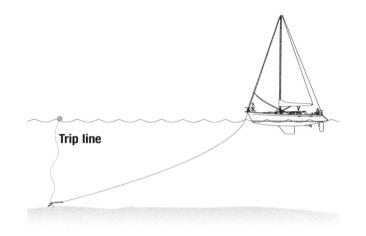

Trip line

## WINDLASS

A windlass is used to raise and/or lower the anchor. Some handle both line and chain, others just chain. They are electrically powered and have a manual backup. To avoid draining the batteries, the engine should be running while using the windlass.

Windlasses are not intended to pull a boat forward against a strong wind or to break the anchor free of the bottom. These actions can trip the circuit breaker, which is often located in a separate location away from the electrical panel.

A power windlass is operated with a button on the deck or a hand control. Keep clothing, hair and other body parts well clear of the gear mechanism. Never put hands on the chain while the power is on.

Winch handle     Windlass     Windlass winch connection

If the windlass fails, the anchor can be raised by hand.

**Be sure your charter briefing is very thorough on windlass operation and always treat it with extreme caution.**

# MEDITERRANEAN (MED) MOORING

Boats save docking space by anchoring with their sterns tied to a fixed pier. A pasarelle (plank) running from the shore to the stern provides access to and from the boat. This procedure, known as Mediterranean, or Med Mooring, requires close coordination between the helm and the crew and should be practiced beforehand. It is a difficult maneuver to perform in a crosswind.

**1** Note the direction of the anchor rodes coming off moored boats. Prepare the anchor rode and stern mooring lines. Place fenders and tie the dinghy to the bow.

**2** Position the boat beyond the anchor rodes already deployed, allowing enough room to regain steering control as you begin backing up.

**3** Lower the anchor, paying out the rode to match your speed.

**4** Let out sufficient scope and snub the rode to set the anchor. Maintain pressure on the rode to keep the boat backing in a straight line.

**5** Just short of touching the dock, cleat the anchor rode. As the rode becomes taut, the windward stern line is passed to a dockhand.

**6** Set a second stern line on the opposite quarter and position the pasarelle.

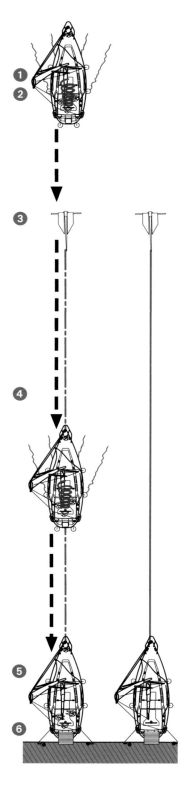

## LAZY LINES (SLIME LINES)

In some charter areas, lazy lines are becoming available. These lines allow you to Mediterranean Moor without having to anchor. The far end of each lazy line is permanently attached to the seabed several boat lengths from the dock. Each of these non-floating lines is then individually laid along the seabed and led to the dock, where the other end is made fast.

To use a lazy line, rig fenders and stern lines as if to Mediterranean Moor in the normal fashion. Back in, but do not deploy your anchor. Have one crew member step onto the dock with a stern line. Have another crew member pick up the lazy line with a boat hook, then walk it forward hand over hand to the bow (yes, it will be slimy!), and secure it as if it were your anchor rode. In some locations you may pick up two lazy lines, one for each bow cleat. There is often someone on the dock to take your stern line and hand you the lazy line.

# PICKING UP A MOORING

Moorings, an alternative to anchoring, are more secure and much easier to use. They are permanently attached to the seabed, often with chain attached to long, screw-like augers into the sand or bolts that are drilled and epoxied into the bedrock. This allows for shorter scope and more boats can be accommodated in the area. Additionally, moorings do much less environmental damage to the seabed than repeated anchoring.

Many charter destinations have moorings available for a fee. The mooring field is often so extensive that it would be difficult to find a safe place to anchor. In some places the mooring is free, but you are expected to eat at the local restaurant or tavern that provided it.

A pendant (a floating line or a line with a float on it) is usually attached to the buoy. You will need to use a boat hook to retrieve the pendant. Occasionally, the pendant will be equipped with a pick-up stick that can be easily reached from the deck. The pendant typically has an eye splice at its end.

**NOTE:** If there is no pendant, a line must be passed through the ring on the buoy. This is best accomplished by a long-armed crew member reaching from the low point of the deck. Take care while motoring near the mooring to not foul it in your prop (See Unfouling a Propeller, p. 129).

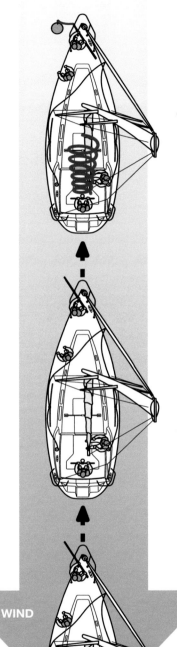

## PICKING UP A MOORING

**3** Use reverse (if necessary) to stop the boat with the bow next to the mooring buoy. Pick up the pendant with the boat hook. Pass the free end of the line through the eye splice and cleat it to the boat. Be careful that the boat hook does not roll off the boat while the line is being secured! If you miss the pendant or the crew cannot hold on, back away slowly or allow the wind to move you clear, and then make another attempt.

**2** Approach the mooring head to wind, shift into neutral and coast slowly up to the mooring buoy.

**WIND**

**1** Cleat a line to one of the bow cleats, make sure it is led outside the bow pulpit, and coil it neatly on the bow. Have a crew member ready at the bow with a boat hook.

# RAFTING UP

Rafting up is tying alongside another boat that is anchored or docked. Sometimes this is done for social reasons or to accommodate many boats in a crowded harbor. You should only raft to another boat with her permission or if instructed to do so by the harbormaster. Successful rafting requires cooperation and mutual consideration.

Both boats should rig all their fenders, except one, high and amidships to protect the topsides. Each boat should keep one as a roving fender to be placed quickly where needed. On the rafting boat, rig bow, stern, and spring lines and assign line handlers.

## RAFTING AT ANCHOR

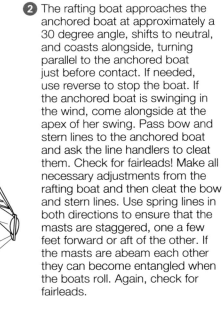

❶ The first boat anchors, rigs fenders, and assigns line handlers.

❷ The rafting boat approaches the anchored boat at approximately a 30 degree angle, shifts to neutral, and coasts alongside, turning parallel to the anchored boat just before contact. If needed, use reverse to stop the boat. If the anchored boat is swinging in the wind, come alongside at the apex of her swing. Pass bow and stern lines to the anchored boat and ask the line handlers to cleat them. Check for fairleads! Make all necessary adjustments from the rafting boat and then cleat the bow and stern lines. Use spring lines in both directions to ensure that the masts are staggered, one a few feet forward or aft of the other. If the masts are abeam each other they can become entangled when the boats roll. Again, check for fairleads.

❸ Readjust bow and stern lines, as needed, to keep the bows angled slightly apart. This way, the wind will tend to hold the boats apart rather than push them together. Confirm that the skipper of the anchored boat is satisfied with the arrangement. Relax!

## RAFTING AT DOCK

❶ The first boat docks, rigs remaining fenders on the outboard side (except for the "roving" fender), and assigns line handlers.

❷ The rafting boat rigs bow, stern, and spring lines and approaches the docked boat at approximately a 30 degree angle, shifts to neutral, and coasts alongside, turning parallel to the docked boat just before contact. If needed, use reverse to stop the boat. Pass bow and stern lines to the docked boat and ask her line handlers to cleat them. Check for fairleads! Make all necessary adjustments from the rafting boat. Cleat the bow and stern lines, and rig spring lines in both directions to ensure that the masts are staggered, one a few feet forward or aft of the other. Again, check for fairleads. Sometimes rafting bow to stern is a practical way to stagger the rigs. If the masts are abeam each other they can become entangled when the boats roll. Once settled, the rafting boat can also rig bow and stern lines directly to the dock for added security.

### RAFTING ETIQUETTE

▶ When crossing a boat, avoid the cockpit. Walk quietly forward of the mast.

▶ Inform other boats of your departure plans.

▶ Be considerate of other people's quiet hours after dark.

# DINGHY AND OUTBOARD MANAGEMENT

When anchored, your dinghy becomes the family car or a bicycle. It will be used to run errands, visit other boats, go snorkeling, and a host of other activities. Your charter company will show you how to start and stop the outboard and explain the company policy regarding towing or stowing aboard.

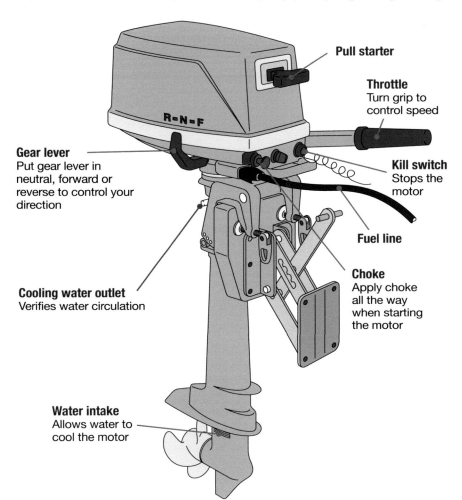

**Pull starter**

**Throttle**
Turn grip to control speed

**Gear lever**
Put gear lever in neutral, forward or reverse to control your direction

R - N - F

**Kill switch**
Stops the motor

**Fuel line**

**Choke**
Apply choke all the way when starting the motor

**Cooling water outlet**
Verifies water circulation

**Water intake**
Allows water to cool the motor

## STARTING PROCEDURE

1. Secure the tilt control lever in the down position.
2. Check for adequate fuel in the tank.
3. Open the fuel tank vent.
4. Check that both ends of the fuel line are securely attached.
5. Pump the bulb firm.
6. Put gear lever in neutral.
7. Pull the choke out.
8. Put the throttle in start position.
9. Pull the starter cord.
10. Push the choke in after engine starts.
11. Check the cooling water outlet.
12. If engine floods, push the choke in, open the throttle all the way and then pull the cord several times. Or, wait several minutes and try again.

---

### SAFETY TIPS

▶ Do not store gasoline (outboard motor fuel) where its fumes can leak into the boat. They will collect in the bilge like water and an errant spark can cause them to explode.

▶ When moving the outboard between the dinghy and its storage location on the stern rail, attach a line and have someone tend it. Dropping the outboard into the water is an expensive error.

▶ Motor slowly through anchorages and around swimmers.

▶ Dinghy equipment should include an anchor, oars or paddles, life jackets, a bailer and a flashlight. Inflatable life jackets satisfy legal requirements only when worn.

Outboard engine should be tied to the dinghy with a safety line.

# UNDERWAY WITH A DINGHY

In open water, tow your dinghy about five or six dinghy lengths astern to clear your wake.

Bring a hard dinghy alongside and use fenders to protect the boat's hull when maneuvering in close quarters. To side tie, use the painter as a bow line and lead a line to the dinghy's stern to secure it alongside.

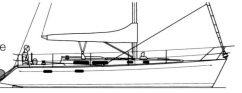

In close quarters, an inflatable may be raised partially against the transom to bring it closer. Make sure it doesn't mar the boat's surface.

## TOWING TIPS

- ▶ Charter company policies about towing vary; be sure you understand them.
- ▶ When towing, remove everything from your dinghy unless otherwise directed by your charter company.
- ▶ If towing the dinghy with the engine attached, tilt it up.
- ▶ Proceed cautiously when towing in high winds or across the wind, waves and wakes to avoid flooding or capsizing the dinghy.
- ▶ Shorten the painter (towline) before slowing or reversing the engine.
- ▶ In close quarters, pull the dinghy up to the stern to keep it out of the way and the painter out of the prop.
- ▶ Double check all knots or use two painters when towing the dinghy.

# LANDING A DINGHY AT A DOCK

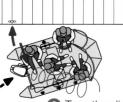

❶ Motor slowly toward the dock at approximately a 45 degree angle.

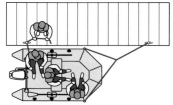

❷ Turn the dinghy and shift to neutral as you reach the dock. Use reverse to stop and bring the stern next to the dock.

❸ Secure the dinghy with bow and stern lines before disembarking.

## BEACH LANDING AND LAUNCHING TIPS

- ▶ Avoid beaches with high surf or rocks.
- ▶ Study the wave pattern and complete your landing or launching in the calmer time between sets.
- ▶ Land bow first with the outboard raised.
- ▶ Carry the dinghy well above the high tide line. Put inflatables in the shade when possible.
- ▶ Launch bow first. Paddle, row or walk it until the outboard can be lowered.

## DINGHY TIPS

- ▶ Secure your dinghy to the dinghy dock with a long bow line so it can be moved aside when others dock.
- ▶ Charter boats look alike in the dark. A light left on or a towel clipped to the lifelines will help ensure you are returning to the correct boat.
- ▶ A flashlight is useful for finding your way in the dark or warning others of your presence. Do not shine your flashlight directly at other people, as it may temporarily blind them.
- ▶ Charter company dinghies are often virtually identical (grey inflatables and black outboards). A handkerchief tied to one of the handles is an easy distinguishing marker.

**NOTE:** At a crowded dock, it may be necessary to use a single bow line and disembark over the bow.

# PROTOCOLS AND LOCAL CUSTOMS

Cruising in foreign countries offers the excitement of meeting people from different cultures. As a guest, your respect for their regulations and way of life will make you welcome. Ignoring or belittling local customs and practices can result in an unfriendly reception. Prepare yourself by learning something about your host country before your trip.

To check in, the boat's captain shows the local officials the boat's documents, passports for each person on board, a crew list, and clearance from the last port.

Upon arrival in a foreign country, fly the yellow Q flag from your starboard spreader until you clear customs, immigration and the port captain. After completing these formalities, lower the Q flag and replace it with the national flag of your host country.

## CHECKLIST

- ► Anchor or moor in a designated area and hoist the yellow Q flag.
- ► Prepare at least three copies of boat papers, crew list, port clearance and equipment declaration.
- ► Captain or owner will go ashore with official papers and all passports while the rest of the crew remain on board.
- ► After clearing, lower the Q flag and replace it with the national flag of your host country.
- ► Before departing, obtain an official clearance for your next port of call.

## Dos and Don'ts

- ► Do learn a few words of the local language.
- ► Do conform with local customs and religions.
- ► Don't attempt to bribe local officials.
- ► Don't take any illegal substances on board. Foreign governments often treat drug offenders with harsh treatment, fines and jail terms.
- ► Do fly the national flag of your boat's registry from the stern when visiting a foreign country.
- ► Do fly the national flag of your host country, also called the courtesy flag, from the starboard spreader.

# NAVIGATION RULES

All vessels are required to comply with the Navigation Rules. Compliance is easier if you know the Rules, or at least those that affect you and the vessel with which you are converging. Please review the Rules as presented in US Sailing's *Basic Cruising* textbook. In addition, the Appendix of *Basic Cruising* has the full text of Rules 1-19, which details the conduct between vessels.

**NOTE:** The U.S. Code of Federal Regulations (33 CFR 88 § 88.05) requires that vessels 12 meters (39.4 feet) or more in length carry a copy of the Inland Rules.

## NAVIGATION LIGHTS

A vessel's navigation lights do much more than just alert you to its presence. The lighting configuration informs you of the vessel's type of propulsion, is an indication of its size, tells you its aspect to you, whether she is stand-on or give-way to you and, sometimes, the nature of its work.

These illustrations show the lights required on a typical charter boat while sailing and motoring. This will allow you to properly identify yourself to others. However, to understand and correctly respond to what you are seeing as you look into the night, you will need to be familiar with (or at least be able to quickly reference) the Navigation Rules.

### UNDER SAIL
**Sidelights** are red on the port side and green on the starboard side, each with an arc of 112.5 degrees. **The sternlight** is white with an arc of 135 degrees. **A tricolor light** combines the red and green port and starboard sidelights with white sternlight for sailboats under 20 meters (65.6 feet). This is not to be used if sidelights and sternlight are lit, or while motoring.

### UNDER POWER
**Sidelights** are red on the port side and green on the starboard side, each with an arc of 112.5 degrees. **The masthead or "steaming" light** faces forward with an arc of 225 degrees. The sternlight is white with an arc of 135 degrees.

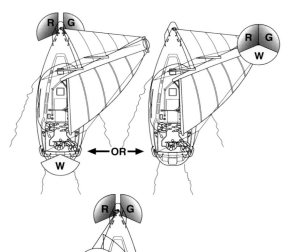

## SOUND SIGNALS

Most ships routinely rely on bridge-to-bridge radio communication to make passing arrangements. This reduces the confusion generated by traditional sound signals in heavy traffic where it may be unclear who is being hailed. Monitoring bridge-to-bridge radio communication is an excellent way to gain awareness of potential ship traffic. Check with your charter company or local knowledge for radio channels used in your area.

A short blast is about a one second in duration and a prolonged blast is from four to six seconds in duration.

● ● ● **Three short blasts** indicate engine is in reverse; a vessel may be backing out of a slip.

● ● ● ● ● **Five short blasts** = danger or doubt.

**Other sound signals:**
▬▬ **One prolonged blast** shall be sounded by a vessel nearing a bend of a channel or fairway where other vessels may be obscured.

For other sound signals (e.g., overtaking signals), consult the Navigation Rules, International-Inland.

## DIVE FLAGS
The white and blue "alpha" code flag is the internationally recognized signal for underwater operations, including a diver in the water. A red flag with a white diagonal stripe is used in U.S. waters to indicate a diver(s) in the water.

# BRIDGES

Bridge clearances (both horizontal and vertical) are printed on the chart. Vertical clearances are measured from Mean High Water; and for opening bridges, given for both the open and closed positions. Know your mast height and check the bridge clearance and state of the tide before attempting to pass under.

Some opening bridges have set schedules and some do not open during rush hour. As you approach, contact the operator (usually Channel 9 on the marine VFH-FM radio) for instructions. Be aware of any tidal current setting you toward the bridge and look for maneuvering room, as you may have to wait.

# LOCKS

Locks are water-filled chambers with water-tight doors at each end. They are used to raise and lower vessels in rivers and canals where the water levels differ.

When the water level in the lock is the same as on the entrance side, the doors will open and you may enter. Once the doors are sealed behind you, the water level in the lock is adjusted (either raised or lowered) until it matches the water level on the exit side. Those doors will then open and allow you to exit the lock.

When the lock is being filled or drained, the water can swirl quite vigorously and large, robust fenders are needed to protect your boat's hull from the rough, grimy lock walls. If there are floating mooring devices that ride up and down the lock walls, the bow and stern can be controlled with short lines. If these devices are not available, two lines, at least twice as long as the vertical range of the lock, are needed to allow crew to tend to the bow and stern lines while on board.

At some locks, there are lock masters to direct traffic and enforce safety procedures, and line handlers to assist you. In other locations (e.g., small, European canals) you will be required to do it all yourself, including the opening and closing of the lock doors and the line handling. Maneuver at slow speeds to minimize your wake, listen for instructions from the lock master, and watch for traffic signals. Flashing red means "Do Not Enter," flashing amber allows for a cautious approach, and green indicates it is safe to enter the lock.

Chapter 4

# CATAMARANS

Catamarans are a popular option for chartering and cruising, particularly for larger groups, families, and anyone who appreciates the great space and privacy of recent designs. A 44-foot catamaran will have considerally more space for accommodations and cabins, compared to a 44-foot monohull. Compare the number of berths not the length of the boat.

For planning purposes, start with the idea that a catamaran designed for charter will offer similar passage times to a monohull boat of the same length. Catamarans designed with performance in mind, on the other hand, may offer passage times at least twice as fast as a comparable monohull.

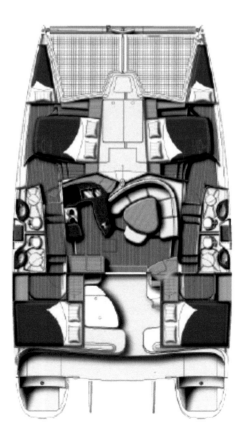

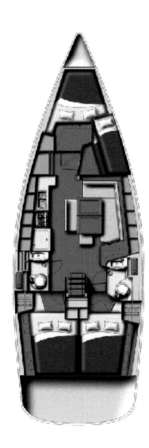

▶ The motion of a catamaran is noticeably different than that of a monohull. A catamaran heels hardly at all, but pitches more, with a motion similar to driving on a bumpy road.

▶ Because a catamaran doesn't heel, the loads on the rig are dramatically higher than on a monohull. For that reason, the weight and strength of the sails and rigging are also significantly greater. Care must be taken, particularly in gusty or rough conditions.

▶ Modern catamarans are so immensely stable that they are very unlikely to capsize, but things may break if the boat is pushed too hard.

# SAILING A CATAMARAN

In many ways, sailing a catamaran is very similar to a monohull, as the majority of sail controls are exactly the same. However, there are some important differences. Catamarans are very sensitive to small sail trim adjustments, which will produce noticeable increases in boat speed. You will need to trim the sails several times (the trim cycle) as the boat speed increases and the apparent wind shifts forward.

## TACKING

Catamarans lack the momentum of monohulls, and sailing just below close-hauled allows them to be fully powered up before tacking. Tack smoothly, with the rudders about halfway over; too much rudder angle will cause them to stall and the boat will not tack. Some catamarans will require the jib to be backwinded in order to complete the tack. When releasing the backed jib, ensure that the new working sheet will not foul on gear at the mast. Ease the main a bit as it begins to fill on the new tack and allow the boat to fall just below close-hauled. Go through the trim cycle as the boat begins to accelerate on the new tack and come back up to close-hauled. In close quarters, consider using the engines.

## JIBING

Catamaran mainsails usually have a large and powerful roach. If not controlled when jibing, the shock loads on the rig are significant. When preparing to jibe, turn downwind until the jib starts to collapse behind the mainsail. Hold course and trim the mainsail to the centerline using both the sheet and traveler. Execute the jibe and ease the mainsail out rapidly.

### CATAMARAN SAILING TIPS

▶ The knotmeter is very useful as a sail trimming tool. It will quickly tell you when you have done something right (or wrong).
▶ While the boom is over the traveler track, use the traveler to trim the mainsail and the mainsheet to adjust twist. All of the leech telltales should be streaming aft, with just the top one tending to curl to leeward.
▶ When hoisting the mainsail, it is easy to snag battens on the lazy jacks. Watch the leech of the mainsail while hoisting. Be cautious when using an electric winch.
▶ Waves slapping against the underside of the bridge deck (sometimes quite loudly) is a normal occurrence in moderate sea conditions.

## Reefing Chart

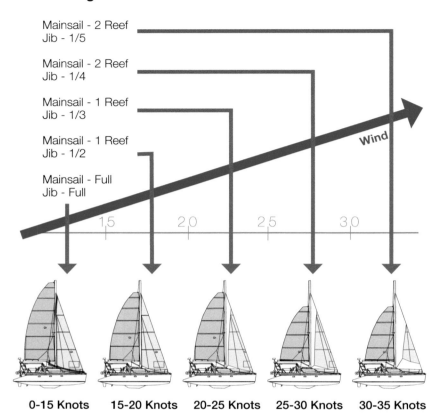

| | 0-15 Knots | 15-20 Knots | 20-25 Knots | 25-30 Knots | 30-35 Knots |

Mainsail - 2 Reef / Jib - 1/5
Mainsail - 2 Reef / Jib - 1/4
Mainsail - 1 Reef / Jib - 1/3
Mainsail - 1 Reef / Jib - 1/2
Mainsail - Full / Jib - Full

15   20   25   30

Wind

## REEFING

The signs that it is time to reduce sail provided by a monohull (e.g., excessive heeling and increasing weather helm) are missing on a catamaran. Because of the lack of heel, the loads on the rig increase dramatically, but the cues are subtler. If the lee shrouds become visibly loose when sailing upwind, it is time to reef. When sailing downwind, watch for a loosening of the diamond shrouds. The process of reefing a catamaran is the same as for a monohull. A catamaran's sail area is set for the gusts, as opposed to a monohull's sail area which is set for the lulls.

The manufacturer or charter company may provide guidance, often in the form of a reefing placard, showing the proper sail configuration for various wind speeds. If this information is not available, ask for it.

# MANEUVERING UNDER POWER

Most charter catamarans have an inboard diesel engine in each hull, with engine controls similar to monohulls. Instead of conventional propeller shafts, some catamarans have saildrives that will reduce or eliminate prop walk. Smaller catamarans may have outboard motors. Some catamarans have their propellers aft of the rudders, significantly affecting prop wash. Start the engine farthest from the helm first so that you can hear it start, and then the one nearer the helm.

These differences in prop walk and prop wash, coupled with the fact that you have twin engines significantly far apart, will make close-quarters maneuvering a catamaran very different than a monohull. At the slow speeds required when operating in close quarters, the rudders are best left centered and the boat maneuvered with the engines only. You are maneuvering a large four-cornered box and you need to keep track of all four corners. It may help to imagine that you are steering a shopping cart. When the helm station is off center, it is helpful to post a lookout on the opposite side.

Because catamarans draw less and have more freeboard than a monohull, strong winds have more effect on a catamaran. As with all sailboats, the bows of a catamaran are pushed downwind more than the sterns. The best (and sometimes the only) way to maneuver a catamaran in strong winds is to back up toward the objective. Going forward may require more power than is comfortable or more room than is available.

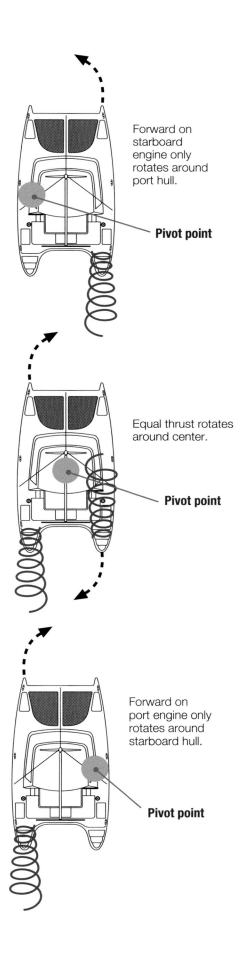

Forward on starboard engine only rotates around port hull.

**Pivot point**

Equal thrust rotates around center.

**Pivot point**

Forward on port engine only rotates around starboard hull.

**Pivot point**

# LEAVING THE DOCK

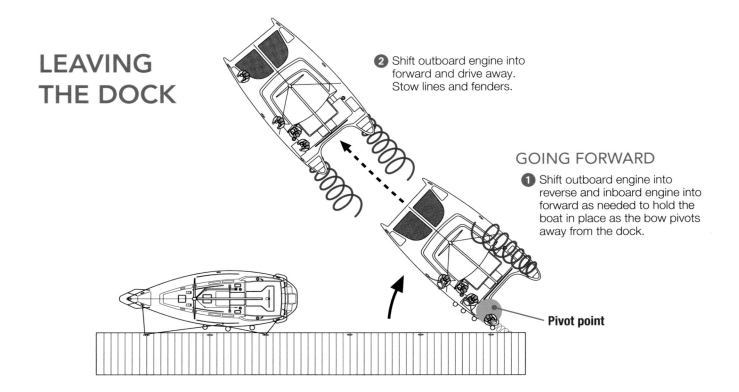

**2** Shift outboard engine into forward and drive away. Stow lines and fenders.

## GOING FORWARD

**1** Shift outboard engine into reverse and inboard engine into forward as needed to hold the boat in place as the bow pivots away from the dock.

**Pivot point**

## CONSIDERATIONS WHEN LEAVING THE DOCK

Secure dinghy on outboard hull or raise on davits. Reposition fenders to protect the topsides when departing. If space is limited, a spring line may be used to hold the boat in position while it is rotated with the engines. Higher topsides on catamarans make doubling spring lines a good option. Release the doubled-back working spring line last as the boat moves away from the dock. Whenever possible, swing out the upwind or upcurrent end of the boat.

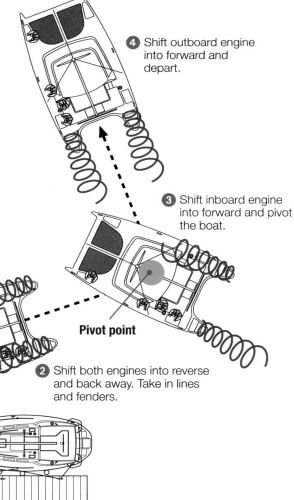

**4** Shift outboard engine into forward and depart.

**3** Shift inboard engine into forward and pivot the boat.

**Pivot point**

## BACKING AWAY

**1** Shift inboard engine into reverse and outboard engine into forward. Pivot the stern away from the dock until the stern is clear.

**Pivot point**

**2** Shift both engines into reverse and back away. Take in lines and fenders.

**Pivot point**

# DOCKING

## CONSIDERATIONS WHEN RETURNING TO THE DOCK

Secure the dinghy onto the outboard hull or raise it onto the davits. Wherever possible, approach into the wind or current, whichever is dominant. Motor slowly past your desired location to check the wind, current and the direction of approach. Return with lines and fenders prepared. If you don't like the space situation or it exceeds your comfort zone, ask the dockmaster for another location. The high freeboard of most charter catamarans will make it necessary to step onto the dock from the stern. For this reason, it may be advantageous to back into the dock. Backing into the dock can also provide better visibility from the helm. Don't be afraid to abandon a docking that's not working and try again.

## DOCKING GOING ASTERN INTO THE WIND AND/OR CURRENT

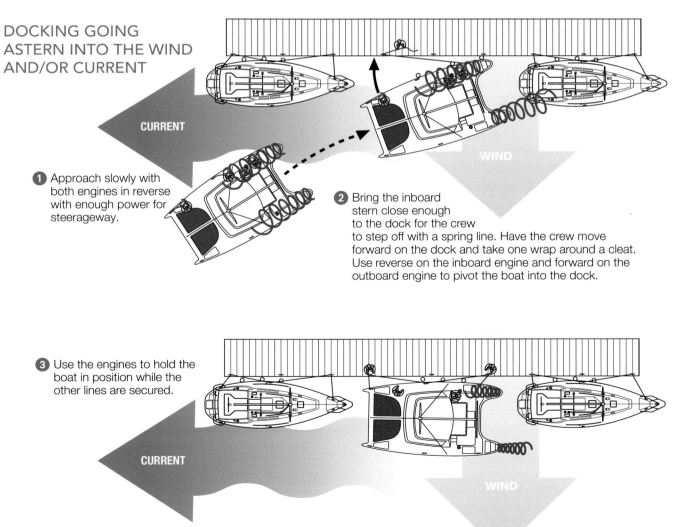

CURRENT

WIND

**1** Approach slowly with both engines in reverse with enough power for steerageway.

**2** Bring the inboard stern close enough to the dock for the crew to step off with a spring line. Have the crew move forward on the dock and take one wrap around a cleat. Use reverse on the inboard engine and forward on the outboard engine to pivot the boat into the dock.

**3** Use the engines to hold the boat in position while the other lines are secured.

CURRENT

WIND

## CROSSWIND DOCKING (WINDWARD SIDE)

The boat's windage will push the catamaran against the dock when approaching the windward side of the dock.

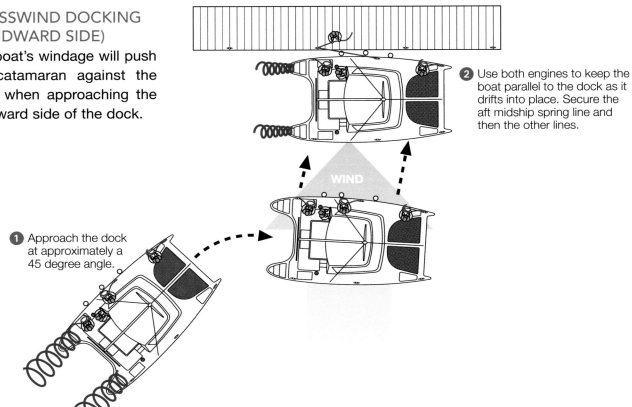

**2** Use both engines to keep the boat parallel to the dock as it drifts into place. Secure the aft midship spring line and then the other lines.

**1** Approach the dock at approximately a 45 degree angle.

WIND

## DOWNWIND DOCKING

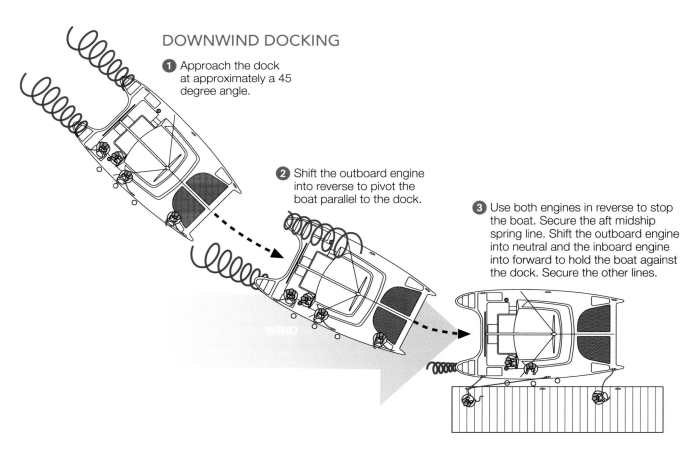

**1** Approach the dock at approximately a 45 degree angle.

**2** Shift the outboard engine into reverse to pivot the boat parallel to the dock.

**3** Use both engines in reverse to stop the boat. Secure the aft midship spring line. Shift the outboard engine into neutral and the inboard engine into forward to hold the boat against the dock. Secure the other lines.

WIND

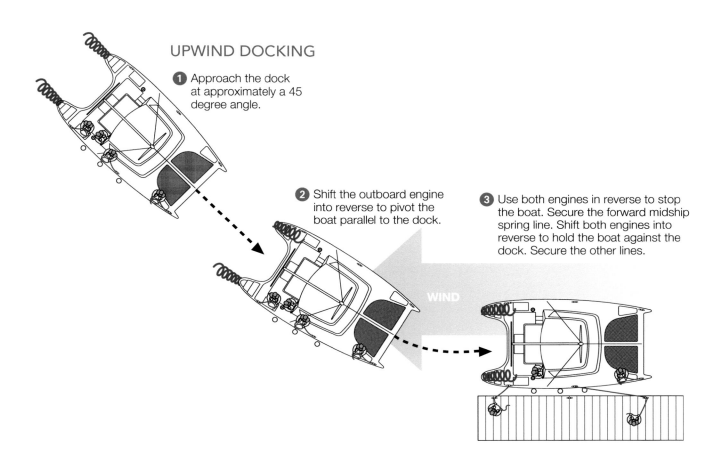

## UPWIND DOCKING

**1** Approach the dock at approximately a 45 degree angle.

**2** Shift the outboard engine into reverse to pivot the boat parallel to the dock.

**3** Use both engines in reverse to stop the boat. Secure the forward midship spring line. Shift both engines into reverse to hold the boat against the dock. Secure the other lines.

WIND

## SECURING THE BOAT

Led from midships, the aft spring line prevents forward motion and the forward spring line prevents motion aft. When securing the boat to a fixed dock in tidal waters, allow for the water level's rise and fall by leading the bow and stern lines to the outboard side.

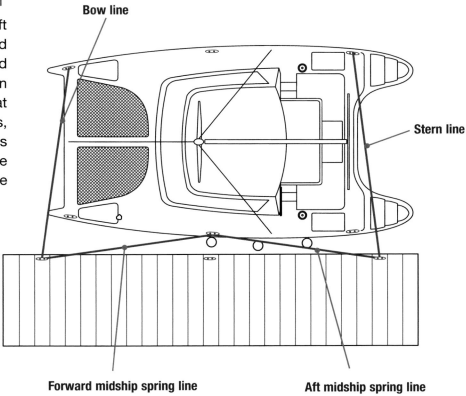

**Bow line**

**Stern line**

**Forward midship spring line**

**Aft midship spring line**

# ANCHORING

One of the real advantages of catamarans is comfort at anchor. Because of their wide beam, catamarans will not roll in chop and small refracted swells. A catamaran can anchor in places that would be uncomfortable, if not untenable, for most monohulls. Their draft allows catamarans to anchor in shallower water than most monohulls.

The basic techniques of anchoring are the same on catamarans as on monohulls. Because catamarans have more windage, they sail around at anchor more. To prevent this, catamarans generally anchor using bridle lines led forward from each hull to the anchor chain. When anchoring, after all of the intended scope is let out, the bridle is attached to the anchor chain. Then more chain is let out so that a large bight of chain hangs into the water and the bridle takes the load.

This prevents the catamaran from sailing around and provides a shock absorber for the chain. A bridle may either be a long line attached to each bow with a hook in the middle or two lines, one running from each bow.

When departing, retrieve the chain until the bridle comes within reach. Remove and stow the bridle, and retrieve the anchor as usual.

When setting two anchors, it may be best to use the dinghy to drop the second anchor. This avoids damaging one or both hulls with the chain.

# MOORING

Catamarans should be attached to the mooring with a bridle. Rig a line from each bow and adjust their length so that the ball cannot reach either hull. Do not use a single line rigged from one bow through the pendant eye and then to the other bow, as this arrangement allows the mooring ball to hit the hull.

## PICK UP AT THE BOW

Rig a bridle line from each bow. Approach the mooring buoy head to wind, stop the boat, and pick up the pendant with a boat hook. Pass each bridle line through the pendant eye, lead it back to its bow, and then secure it.

## PICK UP AT THE STERN

If there is no pendant on the mooring buoy, high freeboard forward will not allow for a bow pickup. The stern steps are the only place from which the mooring buoy can be reached. The steps on the same side as the helm station provide the helmsman with the best view. Rig a bridle line from each bow, and lead both around one side of the boat, outside of everything, to the stern steps. Back into the wind until the crew can pass both bridle lines through the ring on the mooring buoy. Pivot the catamaran while the crew walk the bridle lines to the bows and secure them.

If you don't have a line long enough to reach from the bow to the stern steps on the opposite side, rig the near side one and have a second line available at the stern steps. Once the near side bridle line has been passed through the ring on the mooring ball, hand it to another crew member. Then pass the other bridle line through the ring, keeping both ends in your hands. Both crew members then walk the bridle lines to the bows and secure them.

# STABILITY AND THE ESCAPE HATCH

Modern cruising catamarans are designed to minimize the risk of capsize, even in severe conditions. In the extremely unlikely event of capsize, escape hatches are provided. Modern catamarans are designed to remain afloat whether flooded or inverted.

# Chapter 5

# Navigation

Since the arrival of GPS, with its connected devices in the 1990s, piloting a yacht has undergone a revolution. While a skipper's own eyes remain the most important instruments, modern equipment in sensible hands has made sailing in unfamiliar waters a great deal easier. Despite this, the fundamental duties of the navigator haven't changed since the beginning of seafaring. The two key issues remain the same: "Where am I?" and "How do I pilot the ship safely to my destination?"

GPS answered the first question immediately and the establishment of the electronic chart plotter has had a dramatic effect on the second; but things are not always quite as straightforward as they seem. For safe route planning, an understanding of the timeless principles of navigation is still required. Some basic know-how enables a skipper to stay ahead of the game if the chart plotter should go down or if it delivers answers that are not as safe as a casual glance might suggest. This chapter will guide you through the essentials; it will indicate what today's navigation equipment can do, integrate it with a safe, classical approach, and warn about circumstances where special care is required.

## THE CHART

### THE PAPER CHART

Keeping a yacht on track during short coastal passages usually involves a marine equivalent of orienteering rather than plotting in the traditional way with pencil and rulers. This type of piloting has its own set of skills, beginning with the ability to read a paper chart. The paper chart underpins all knowledge of the environment in which you are sailing, and most electronic charts draw their data from the same sources. Electronic charts may not always show you everything you need to know without making adjustments to the display.

## ORIENTATION

The vast majority of charts is in North-up format, meaning that North is at the top; West is at the left, East is to the right, and South is at the bottom. If you ever become disoriented out on the water, glance at the steering compass, note where North is, and swivel the chart around to coincide.

Some believe that a paper chart should never be brought on deck for fear of losing or damaging it. However, when proper precautions are taken, having a paper chart or cruising guide available at the helm can be useful, especially when entering or leaving port. If necessary, protect it from rain or spray with a plastic bag and ensure that it does not blow away.

## CHART SYMBOLS

Many chart symbols are self-explanatory, such as those for buoys, radio masts, chimneys, churches, bridges and wrecks. Note that floating buoys are always shown at a jaunty angle, while beacons stand vertically. All yachts should carry a copy of *U.S. Chart No. 1*, the bible of chart symbols. Available as a free download, this is also available in hard copy as a booklet.

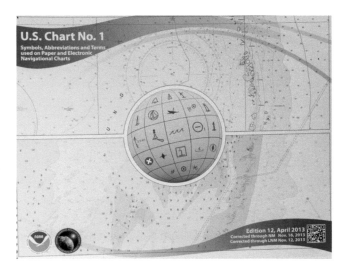

## SCALE ON A PAPER CHART

The scales on both sides of the chart represent latitude in degrees (0-90 North or South of the Equator). Each degree is divided into 60 minutes. Because one minute of latitude equals one nautical mile or about 2000 yards (1852 meters), this scale is used to measure distance. Depending on the scale, minutes may be further divided in half, into 10ths of minutes, or into seconds (60ths).

The scales running across both the top and bottom denote longitude. Never use this for distance because degrees of longitude vary in size considerably between mid-latitudes, the equator and the poles. They subdivide in the same manner as degrees of latitude and serve to cross-reference a position so it can be expressed in two dimensions.

## SCALE ON A CHART PLOTTER

On a chart plotter, you rarely display an entire chart because you would not be able to decipher anything, due to the small screen size. Because the latitude and longitude scales are not available for defining position or measuring distance, chart plotters handle these functions differently. Typically, the unit will have a data box that displays the latitude and longitude of the vessel. There will be other data boxes that show the latitude and longitude of the cursor's location on the chart as well as the range and bearing to that location. Measuring distance on a chart plotter is simply a matter of positioning the cursor and reading the distance in the appropriate data box. Bringing your own tablet preloaded with charts will make navigation simpler.

## TITLE BLOCK

The title block includes chart datum, scale and measurement units for soundings and heights. The chart's issue date, along with any corrections, are located in bottom left corner. Keep current charts on board and update them with Local Notices to Mariners changes.

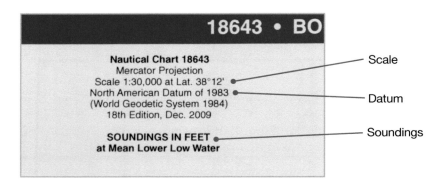

## DEPTHS

To move about the watery parts of our world, we must know if the water is deep enough for us to do so safely. The chart supplies this information in the form of numbers which represent soundings or the depth of the water at that location. The title block tells us what units are being used on that chart, (e.g., feet, fathoms [6 feet], fathoms and feet, or meters). This information is also printed in bold magenta capital letters in several places along the margins of the chart.

If the chart is in fathoms and feet, the main number is in fathoms and the subscript is in feet, so $4_3$ represents 4 fathoms (6x4=24 feet) plus 3 feet for a total depth of 27 feet. On a metric chart, $4_3$ represents 4.3 meters. In tidal waters you will also see soundings with a line under them. They look like this, $\underline{5}$, and are drying heights. Think of the line as chart datum (MLLW), so this spot dries (or emerges from the water) when the tide is a positive 5 feet.

Charted depths are referenced to the Chart Datum. On U.S. charts, this is Mean Lower Low Water (MLLW), a level based on the mean of the lowest daily water level over an almost 19-year period. This means that there are times when there will be LESS water than is shown on the chart. Many European charts use Lowest Astronomical Tide (LAT), the theoretical minimum predicted by tide tables.

In areas of minimal tidal change, a few charting authorities reference depths to a mid-tidal datum. Other charting agencies use different datums; the title block on each chart will provide the information you need. Always check on a new chart to be sure. Be aware that extreme barometric pressures and strong prolonged winds can alter predicted depths significantly.

## CONTOURS AND BOTTOM

The depths on paper charts are organized around contour lines, which connect locations of equal depth. There are often different shades or colors between contour lines: white is the deepest water; green denotes areas that cover and uncover with the tides; and shades of blue are used for those depths in between. These colors make reading the chart much easier. Small letters indicate the nature of the sea bed. Examples include mud (M), sand (S), clay (Cy), coral (Co), rocky (Rk; rky) and kelp (K).

## HEIGHTS

On U. S. charts, the shoreline at Mean High Water (MHW) is shown as a solid heavy black line. This is the datum from which heights are measured. This includes the height of a light or hill and the clearance under a bridge.

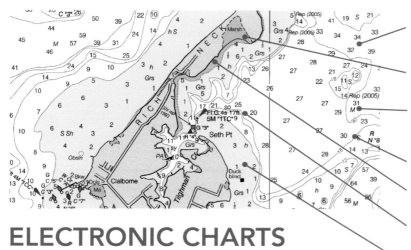

# ELECTRONIC CHARTS

## RASTER SCAN CHARTS

Electronic Navigation Charts (ENCs) come in two formats. The raster scan chart, usually referred to a raster, is effectively a scan of the equivalent NOAA paper chart. It contains all of the notes and ancillary data found on these, including survey data which can help you decide how much reliance to put on super-accurate GPS.

Many people find rasters easy to read because they look exactly like a paper chart on a screen and can be used with chart plotter programs. Some commercial plotters accommodate them. If yours does not, consider loading them on a PC.

Because of its paper chart ancestry, a raster chart cannot be zoomed like a vector chart (see below). What you see is what you get, meaning that they are not subject to the layering issues inherent in vector charts. If you want more detail, shift to a more useful scale of chart, which is typically a one-click function once downloaded. NOAA raster charts are available as free downloads and cover all U.S. home waters.

## VECTOR CHARTS

These are electronic navigation charts commonly found in commercial chart plotters and are derived from vectorized survey data. The data are packaged into what is really an enormous chart containing everything known about an area of the ocean. Used properly, they make life easy. Abused, and boats end up on reefs.

## Chart Features

The numbers scattered throughout the water are soundings at mean lower low water.

Green indicates area that cover and uncover with the tide.

Letters indicate the nature of the seabed, such as mud (M), sand (S), clay (Cy), coral (Co) and rocky (Rk; rky).

A contour line follows a constant water depth.

The thick solid black line indicates the shoreline at Mean High Water.

The number "17" indicates the height of the light above Mean High Water.

Light blue indicates areas of shallower water.

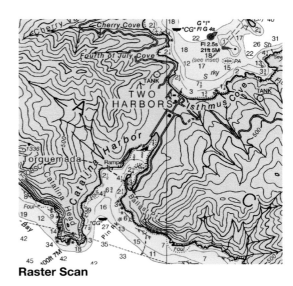

**Raster Scan**

**Vector Chart**

## ZOOMING AND PANNING ISSUES

Whether viewed on a PC or a commercial plotter, all ENCs suffer from the fact that the screen isn't large enough. Zooming and panning an ENC is the magnification to reveal more detail and shunting what you are seeing sideways to discover what is off the screen.

There is more to zooming a vector chart than might meet the eye. Because the chart is carrying far more information than can be displayed on a small screen, the data are reduced to layers. As the area we need for plotting a course appears on the screen, some details disappear. By the time a whole day's passage is in the frame, few specifics may remain at all. As detail is layered out, vital dangers can vanish, only to be found again by zooming. This can be tedious, as a sailboat doesn't often trundle down the rhumb line like a motor cruiser. To discover what might or might not be lurking in the way, the paper chart or its raster equivalent needs to be referenced. Sensible modern piloting uses both formats for overview, detail, and to see the boat's position at any given time.

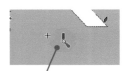

The greenish brown color indicates an area of shallow water surrounding the lighthouse.

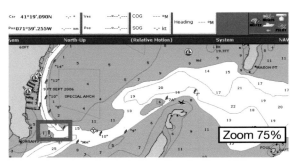

An electronic chart zoomed in tightly – note that this provides a lot of useful close-in detail, but the over-view is nonexistent.

The same lighthouse shown above indicates no shallow water.

The same chart zoomed out for overview – note the lack of useful detail.

## INTERROGATING A VECTOR CHART

A further issue with many vector charts is also tied up with the amount of data that can be shown at one time. On most scales, what you will see is a simplified picture of what's actually there. For example, a channel may be shown as defined by red and green marks. All you see is red and green blobs. To know what one of these may be, you must hover a cursor over it and click. Full data will then pop up, indicating that it is a buoy or beacon, what its light characteristics may be, and so on. This technique may even apply to spot depths, bottom characteristics, and all manner of further information which may not be immediately apparent without interrogation.

## SONAR CHARTS

Certain chart manufacturers encourage crowd-sourced data to be incorporated into their charts, thus creating a sonar chart. While they do have their uses, many are not to be used for navigation since certain information may be left out to allow for the additional contour lines. The navigation chart will be available at a click, as long as you are familiar with the menus. Don't be seduced by sonar charts where they are inappropriate.

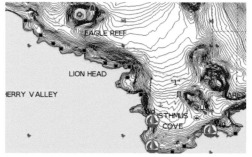

**Sonar Charts**

## THE PERSONAL CHART PLOTTER

Chart plotters on typical charter boats are often sited low down in the cockpit, making them difficult to read, especially in bright sunlight. Also, any instrument is only as good as the user's skill. Strange plotters can soak up several hours before new skippers have all the possibilities at their fingertips. There's a lot to be said, therefore, for taking your own plotter on a charter.

Chart kits with basic plotter software to run on smartphones or, more usefully, tablets, are readily available. Smartphones are convenient but the screen is too small for real navigation. Tablets can be very successful and all have the huge advantage that you, the user, can give yourself plenty of time to learn how they can deliver their best. Seasoned veterans frequently arrive for a charter with a tablet in their kitbag, loaded with the latest charts. The cost is relatively low, and they have probably already had fun creating virtual passages in their chosen area(s) and are completely familiar with their plotter's capabilities.

Provided with a paper chart beside it, a tablet is a boon when piloting through close quarters; this will afford you the ability to keep an eye on the overview. Because plotter charts will be vectors, the paper backup will guard against any layering issues that may inadvertently arise. It will also save you from the tyranny of interrogation required by some charts to discover whether a marker is a buoy, a beacon, or perhaps even a lighthouse.

navionics®

## GPS AND CHART PLOTTER - EXPECTATIONS OF ACCURACY

The chart plotter you may find on a charter boat is a unit containing software to drive ENCs and navigation programs. Although not always the case, the charts may be supplied by an external company. The position factor is supplied by GPS. The GPS receiver and associated software is often integral with the plotter, but it may be external to it.

Whether it is in the plotter, an outside antenna-based unit, or a stand-alone GPS receiver with its own readout, any GPS is subject to issues, some of which are inherent. Others can be adjusted in the settings. The latter would be no issue on your own boat because you would set it up once and for all. If someone else set up the charter boat plotter, take a good look at it.

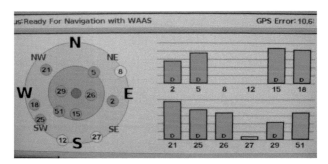

This GPS satellite screen indicates that signals are being received from nine satellites and the accuracy of the GPS position is estimated as 10.6 feet. Four satellites are needed for a 3D fix (position and altitude). The position and number of satellites will vary as the earth rotates and the satellites change their positions in orbit. Satellite signals cannot penetrate solid objects. If used below deck in a boat, an external antenna may be needed.

## GPS ACCURACY

### GPS AND CHARTING

Before electronics came along, charts were accurate within the limits of the compasses and leadlines upon which navigators relied. With GPS offering potential accuracy to within three decimal points of a minute of latitude, it is far ahead of most practical charting. This means that care is needed before placing too much reliance on positions whose circle of accuracy is less than the length of a boat.

### DATUM SHIFTS

An ENC will almost always be accurate in terms of how one shore feature relates to another, so it is natural to assume that the boat sailing across the chart is placed equally precisely. This is generally true in home waters, but situations can occasionally go awry.

GPS thinks in lat/long. The graticule of lat/long lines over our charts has been placed according to a protocol. Across much of the planet, this is the World Geodetic System 1984, or WGS84. Some authorities, however, used different datums to draw their charts and not all have been brought into line with the modern world.

These can slip through the cracks of the software and ENC builders, leaving a perfectly accurate WGS84 fix showing the boat in the wrong position on the plotter. If in any doubt about the GPS position, it pays to back it up with a compass bearing or two and a depth sounding. This policy lines up with classical navigating philosophy, by which nobody was ever satisfied with a position until confirmed by at least one alternative source of data.

# GPS AND CHART PLOTTER SETTINGS

## UNITS OF POSITION

Devices offer a variety of units for defining and displaying position. It is important to ensure the instrument is set up to your liking. The most universal units are degrees, minutes, and tenths of minutes; most chart scales read this way. Other options include the 'older' degrees, minutes, and seconds which divided a minute into 60 seconds, and the 'modern' degrees and decimals of a degree which lacks the convenience of one minute of latitude equaling one nautical mile and is not used in marine navigation.

## DIRECTION SETTINGS

Devices can give direction in either degrees True or Magnetic. The difference between these two readings is called Variation and can be as great as 15 degrees or more, so don't assume anything. Make sure that your device is set to the one you prefer.

## DISTANCE, SPEED AND TIME

Distance (D) is measured in nautical miles. One nautical mile is defined as one minute of latitude which equals approximately 6076 feet or 2000 yards. It is divided into tenths. This is the universal unit of distance for sailors, but devices can be set to statute miles or kilometers. Be sure you check!

Speed (S) is measured in knots. The knot is defined as one nautical mile per hour and is the marine standard for speed. It is expressed in knots and tenths of knots.

Time (T) is measured in hours, which are divided either into tenths or into minutes.

The relationship among these three components is expressed in the following three formulas:
$D = S \times T$; $T = D / S$; and $S = D / T$ (for an answer in hours and 1/10s of hours) or $S = 60 \times D / T$ (for an answer in minutes).

## DEAD RECKONING

These relationships allow us to plot a vessel's position based on the direction steered and the distance sailed. This distance may be obtained by the formula $D = S \times T$, or read directly from the ship's log, which is the equivalent of an odometer. This is known as dead reckoning (DR).

## TIME

A chart plotter's or a GPS's internal clock can be set to several datums (e.g., UTC, your local watch time, Daylight Saving Time). In nontidal waters, this isn't very important. However, if you are using tidal data supplied by your chart plotter, it is essential that the chart plotter's internal clock corresponds to the time in the area in which you are sailing. A difference of even an hour could be significant.

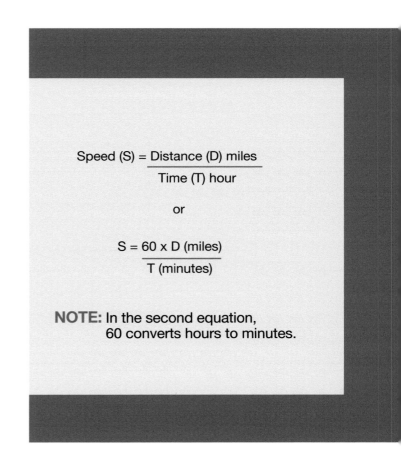

$$\text{Speed (S)} = \frac{\text{Distance (D) miles}}{\text{Time (T) hour}}$$

or

$$S = \frac{60 \times D \text{ (miles)}}{T \text{ (minutes)}}$$

**NOTE:** In the second equation, 60 converts hours to minutes.

# DIRECTION

## THE COMPASS

At sea and on the chart, direction is defined in 360 degree notation. For example, due north is 000 degrees and due south is 180 degrees. All compass bearings are given in three figures to remove any confusion that might arise from, for example, ninety being mistaken for nineteen. Ninety degrees (090°) is, therefore, spoken as zero-nine-zero.

## COURSE

Courses are given in the direction of travel.

## BEARING

The bearing is the direction to an object.

## TRUE AND MAGNETIC BEARINGS AND HEADINGS

True North is the direction of the geographic North Pole. A magnetic compass orients itself to the Earth's magnetic field, creating a difference called Variation. The compass rose on a paper chart shows direction in degrees True on the outer ring and Magnetic on the inner ring. Either can be used when plotting. A GPS may be set to either one. Always label a course or bearing with a suffix T for True or M for Magnetic so there is no confusion.

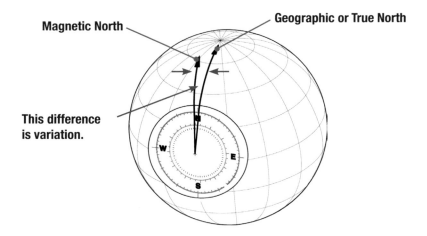

The amount of variation changes very slowly over time. The rate of change is indicated on the compass rose. GPS units allow for the change automatically.

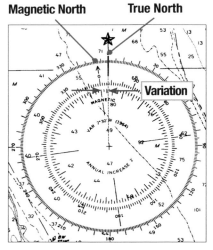

Variation can be either East or West. This example shows Magnetic North to the West of True North and is a West variation. The note inside the circles indicates a variation of 7° 30″ W (West).

# AIDS TO NAVIGATION

Sailors have been creating and using aids to navigation for millennia, from a stick stuck in the mud at a shallow spot to the Lighthouse of Alexandria. Unfortunately, these systems evolved independently from each other. As worldwide voyaging became more common, the different systems in use around the world created confusing and often dangerous situations for mariners. The International Association of Marine Aids to Navigation and Lighthouse Authorities (IALA), created in 1957, has reduced what was more than 30 systems to two, called System A and System B. System B is used in all of North, South and Central America, the Caribbean, South Korea, Japan, Taiwan and the Philippines. System A is used everywhere else.

Floating aids are called buoys and range in size from massive 40-foot high structures to a painted plastic jug. Aids constructed on land or the seabed (nonfloating) are called beacons and can be as simple as a telephone pole driven down into the sea bottom or as massive as the classical lighthouse.

System A

System B

The International Association of Marine Aids to Navigation and Lighthouse Authorities System A and System B.

## LATERAL MARKS

These are red and green and mark the sides or edges of channels. This is the only place where the two systems differ. In System B (the U.S. system), red aids are left to starboard when sailing into a harbor (RED, RIGHT, RETURNING) and green aids are left to port. In System A, it is just the opposite; green aids are left to starboard and red aids to port when approaching the land. Both systems number these marks for identification purposes. When lighted, red buoys show red lights and green buoys show green lights.

## PREFERRED CHANNEL MARK

When a channel divides, a preferred channel mark will be placed in the fork. These are horizontally banded red and green marks; the top color denotes the preferred channel (e.g., wider, deeper, main harbor) and the lower color denotes the secondary channel (e.g., the marina or yacht club).

Depending on which side of the fork is the preferred channel, either color can be on top. They show a letter(s) for identification purposes. When lighted, the light is the same as the top color of the buoy and the flashing pattern is 2+1 (two short flashes followed by a pause, and one more short flash).

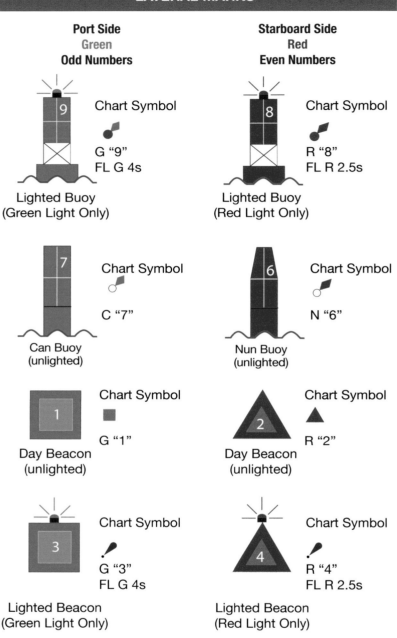

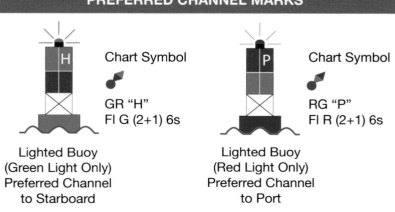

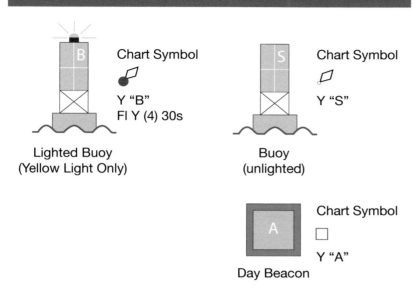

## SPECIAL MARKS

These are solid yellow marks and may show a yellow X as a topmark. They are intended to indicate features like recreation zones, construction sites, or mooring areas. Data acquisition buoys are classified as special marks and are also yellow. When lighted, the light is yellow.

## ISOLATED DANGERS

These are horizontally banded red and black marks with two spherical topmarks one above the other. They are not assigned numbers, but may be lettered. When lighted, the light is white and flashes twice in rapid succession, followed by a longer pause. Consult the chart to find the location of the danger in relation to the mark.

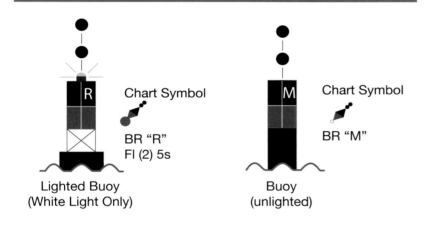

## SAFE WATER MARKS

These are vertically striped red and white marks with one spherical, red topmark. They are used in one of two ways: to mark the seaward end of a channel (often called the sea buoy); or to mark the center of a channel. In either case, they will show a letter(s) for identification purposes. When lighted, the light is white. In the United States, the pattern will be Morse Code A (a short flash followed by a long flash). Elsewhere, other patterns are used.

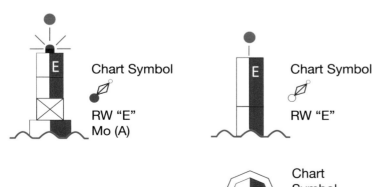

# REGULATORY AND INFORMATIONAL MARKS

These are white with orange bands above and below various symbols. The square indicates information, the circle for controlled areas, and the diamond for danger and exclusion areas.

Diamond
shape warns
of danger

Diamond shape
with cross means
boats keep out

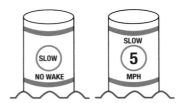

Circle marks
area controlled
"as indicated"

Square displays information
such as directions,
distances and locations

# RANGES

Ranges are based on the geometric principle that any two points define a line. They are unambiguous and keeping a boat on course requires no special instruments, only the navigator's eyes. If the range markers remain in alignment, the boat is on course. Naturally occurring ranges have been used by mariners for millennia, and we have been constructing them for almost as long.

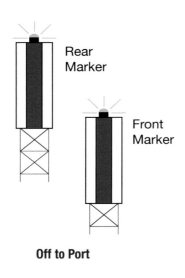

**Off to Port**

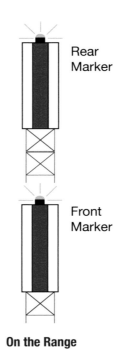

**On the Range**

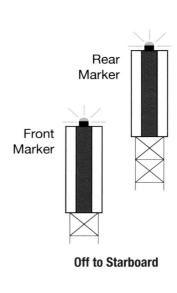

**Off to Starboard**

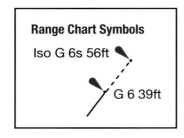

**Range Chart Symbols**

Iso G 6s 56ft

G 6 39ft

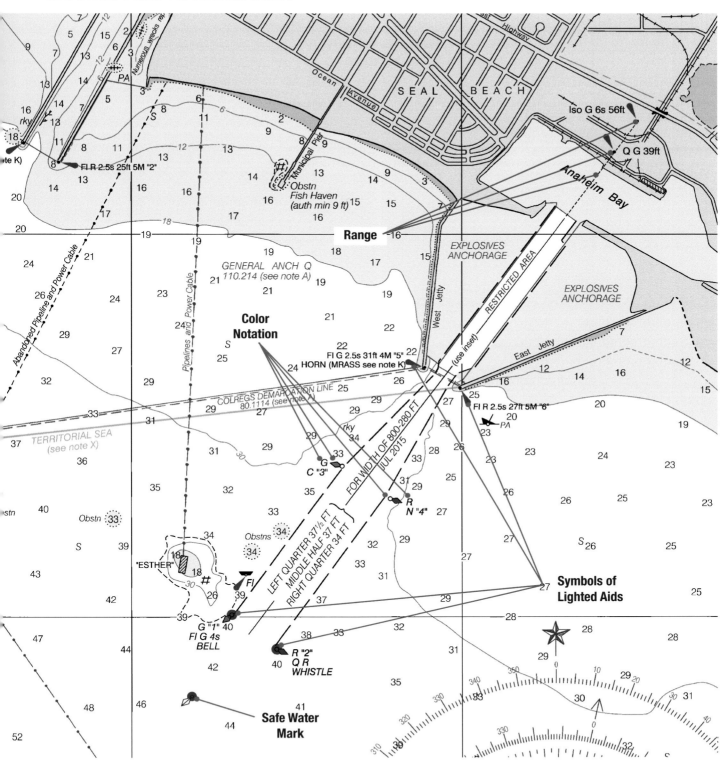

This chart displays a variety of Aids to Navigation, including lighted buoys, lighted beacons, a safe water mark, and a range.

# THE INTRACOASTAL WATERWAY

Sailors on both the United States East and Gulf Coasts should be aware of the Intracoastal Waterway (ICW), commonly referred to as "The Ditch." This protected waterway uses its own unique yellow markings which are placed on regular aids to navigation. By convention, "Clockwise Around America" (southbound on the Atlantic Coast, north or westbound on the Gulf Coast, and northbound on the Pacific Coast) has been designated as "in." Therefore, the ICW uses yellow triangles to mark the continental (mainland) side and yellow squares to mark the seaward side of the ICW. This is true regardless of the color of the navigation aid on which they appear.

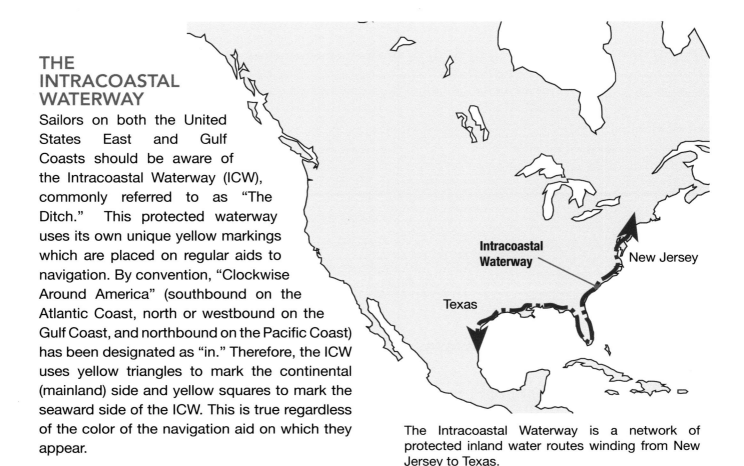

The Intracoastal Waterway is a network of protected inland water routes winding from New Jersey to Texas.

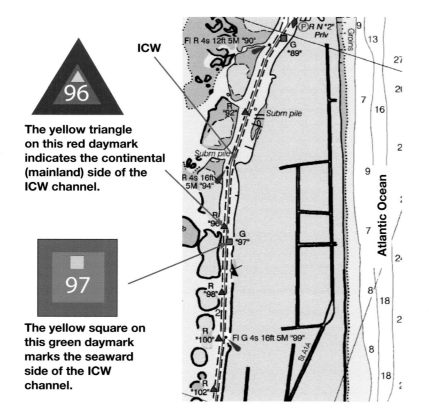

The yellow triangle on this red daymark indicates the continental (mainland) side of the ICW channel.

The yellow square on this green daymark marks the seaward side of the ICW channel.

There are many places where the ICW crosses (and sometimes runs along with) a ship channel leading in from the sea. If the "in" direction of the ICW coincides with the "in" direction of the ship channel, then the ICW's yellow triangles will appear on the ship channel's red aids and the ICW's yellow squares on the ship channel's green aids. However, if the "in" direction of the ICW does not coincide with the "in" direction of the ship channel, then the ICW's yellow triangles will be placed on the ship channel's green markers and the yellow squares on the ship channel's red aids. The mixture of marks can be very confusing. The prudent navigator will examine charts closely, carry an up-to-date ICW cruising guide, and consult it frequently.

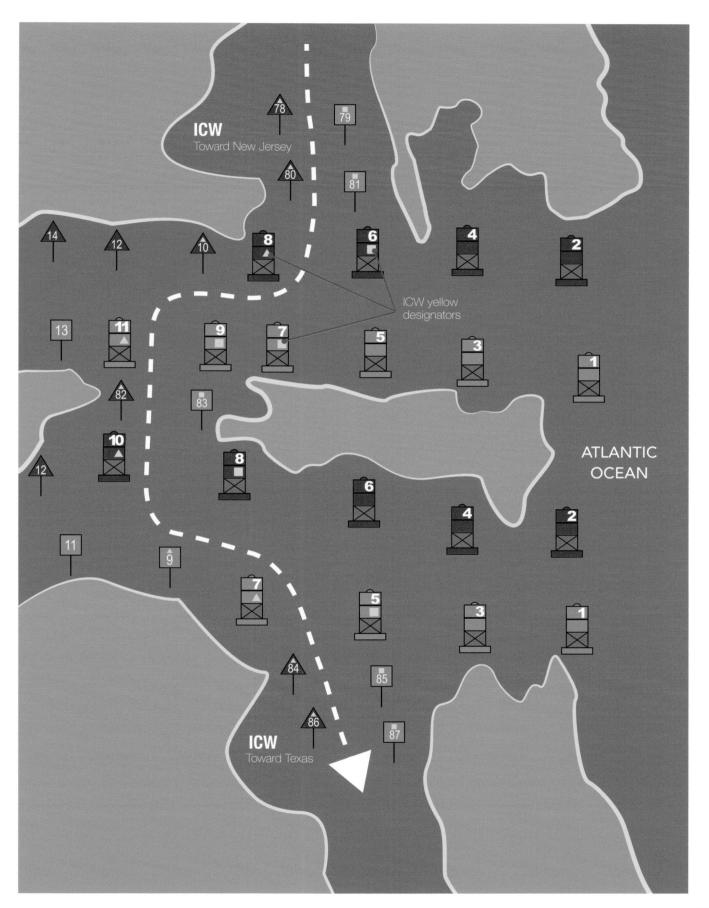

## CARDINAL MARKS

There are four cardinal marks, each named for a cardinal point of the compass: North; South; East; and West. For example, a North cardinal mark stands to the north of the danger, and an East cardinal mark to the east of the danger. An advantage of this mark is that you know the safe side without having to consult the chart for context.

Cardinal marks display black and yellow horizontal bands in a variety of patterns. The triangular black topmarks point to the location of the black band or bands as follows:

**North:** Both topmarks point upward – the black band at the top and the yellow band at the bottom. When lighted, the light is white and will be Quick Flashing or Very Quick Flashing.  Chart symbol: BY

**East:** Topmarks point up and down with their bases together – the black bands at the top and bottom with a yellow band between them. When lighted, the light is white and flashes a group of three. Chart symbol: BYB

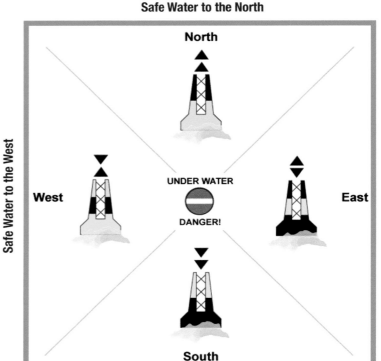

**West:** Topmarks point up and down with their points together – the black band in the middle with yellow bands on the top and bottom. When lighted, the light is white and flashes nine times. Chart symbol: YBY

**South:** Both topmarks point downward – the black band at the bottom and the yellow band at the top. When lighted, the light is white, and flashes six times followed by a long flash. Chart symbol: YB

# DEPTH

## DEPTH SOUNDERS

Any depths given on chart plotters or paper charts are charted depths at chart datum level, not the real-time depth being delivered by the boat's depth sounder. If set up accordingly, some chart plotters have the capacity to show the real sounded depth in a side box. The only true arbiter of depth is the depth sounder. In the final stages of coming in to anchor, this is what you will be looking at, not the chart or the chart plotter.

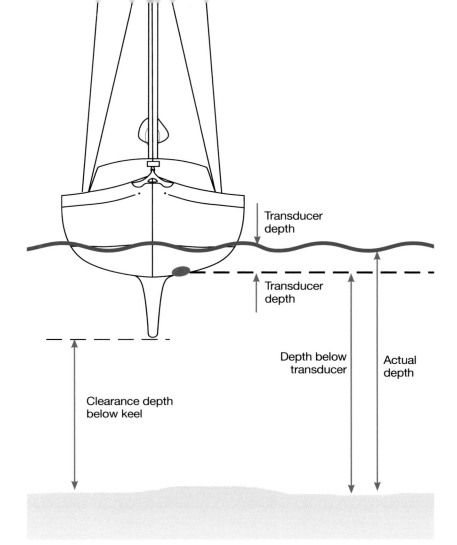

## DEPTH UNITS

It is helpful to set the depth sounder to read out in the same units as the chart plotter or the paper chart. This may be meters, fathoms, feet, or fathoms and feet. Make sure you are clear about the units; expensive mistakes have been made.

## CALIBRATION

Depth sounders can be calibrated to read depth below keel, actual depth of water, and depth below transducer (see illustration above). Charter companies may set the sounder to read depth below keel as a last-ditch tool to stop you from running aground. In any case, the charter before you may have changed the setting and it is good practice to confirm its readout before departure. Simply measure the depth of the water in the slip with a weighted line, and compare it to the readout. Remember: a known error is as good as accurate.

## CHART SYMBOLS FOR HAZARDS

Underwater hazards are shown in a variety of ways. All symbols are explained in *U.S. Chart No. 1*.

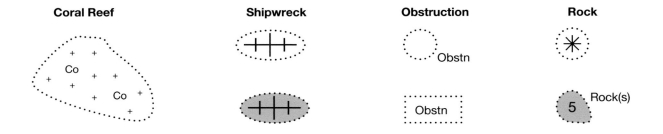

## TIDAL HEIGHTS

When the Sun and Moon are aligned with the Earth (Full and New Moon), their gravities combine to create higher High Tides and lower Low Tides, called Spring Tides. When the Sun and Moon are at right angles with respect to the Earth (the first and last quarters), their gravities create more moderate tides, called Neap Tides.

If you are chartering in an area with significant tidal range, the charter company should issue you a set of tide tables or an almanac containing this data. Typically, the times and heights of high and low water are tabulated. Remember that all tidal heights are to be added to the charted depths, unless they are given as negative figures, in which case they are subtracted.

Some tide table books contain a graph and a set of instructions to guide you to the height of tide at any given moment. Not everybody finds these calculations simple, but anyone can work up the tide height by using the program built into most plotters. If in doubt about how to do this, ask before you leave, but the usual method is to select an icon near a tide station and click on it; up pops a tide graph with a cursor that can be moved to predict tides to the minute, even on a different day.

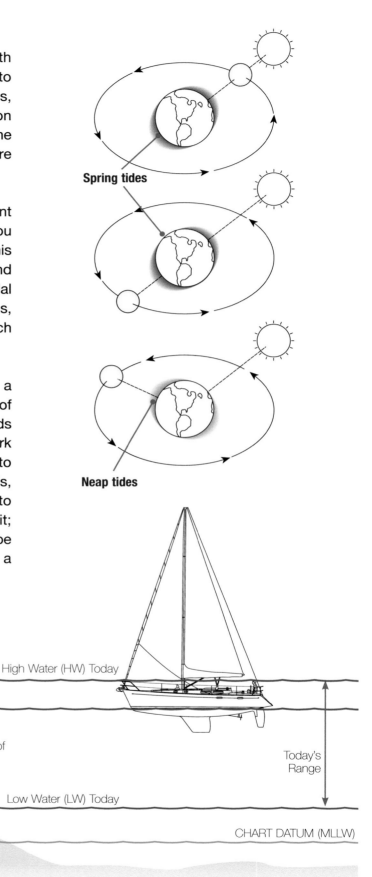

Spring tides

Neap tides

High Water (HW) Today

Current Water Level

Rise of Tide

Today's Range

Height of Tide

Low Water (LW) Today

Drying Height

CHART DATUM (MLLW)

## THE RULE OF TWELFTHS

Tide does not rise or fall at the same rate over its entire cycle. Whether rising or falling, the change starts slowly, speeds up during the middle of the cycle, and slows again toward the end. The Rule of Twelfths will help you determine the height of a tide at any time during the cycle. While this rule is convenient, remember that it is only an approximation and you need to maintain adequate clearance under your keel.

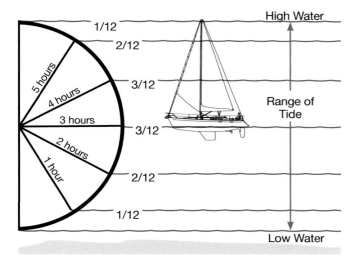

## TIDAL CURRENTS

The rise and fall of the tide causes horizontal water flow called tidal current. The direction in which the current flows is called the Set of the current and the speed of the current is called the Drift. The drift of tidal current can vary significantly in different places around the world and locally over very short distances. Because of the small tidal range in the Mediterranean, the tidal currents are almost nonexistent. In Southeast Alaska, where tidal change can exceed 10 meters (~33 feet), tidal currents can reach 15 knots. If the flow of the current is forced through a small opening (called a Tidal Gate), its velocity can increase rapidly over a short distance.

When sailing in tidal waters, an understanding how to utilize tidal current predications is essential to safe navigation. Even a moderate current of three or four knots can have a substantial impact on the vessel's position or the time it takes to complete a passage.

## TIDAL CURRENT PREDICTIONS

Tidal current predictions are available in both electronic and printed formats. Many chart plotters have tidal current programs built into their software. Once you have learned how to access this data, the program should allow you to scroll forward to find the times that are favorable for your planned passage.

Printed versions may list only the time of Slack Water and the time and velocity of the Maximum Ebb and Flood, leaving you to interpolate for intermediate times. Other versions are in the form of hourly tidal current charts, which make it very easy to find the direction and velocity of any time of the tidal current at intermediate times.

### THE RULE OF THIRDS

To approximate the velocity of the current at intermediate times, divide the time from Slack to Max (or Max to Slack) into three equal time periods. One third of the way from Slack to Max the current will be approximately 50% of the total maximum predicted velocity. At two thirds of the way from Slack to Max, the current will be approximately 90% of the predicted maximum velocity. One third of the way from Max to Slack, the current will be approximately 90% of the predicted maximum velocity. At two thirds of the way from Max to Slack, the current will be approximately 50% of the predicted maximum velocity.

## A WORD OF CAUTION

Once you have learned how to access and utilize tide and current data, you will find them to be your friend, not your nemesis. Passages will be swifter, often more comfortable, and arrivals will be in the daylight instead of the dark.

Remember, both tide and tidal current information are predictions, not promises! Unexpected and extreme weather conditions can alter these predictions substantially. Mistakes in the data have been made in the past and may be made in the future. A prudent sailor doesn't rely solely on a single piece of information but is always looking for confirming data and always trying to reconcile for any piece of data that is at odds with the rest.

## READING CURRENT

Running aground is a serious consequence of being offset by a current. Each time you pass by a fixed object in the water, observe the Set and Drift of the current.

The three-knot current shown pushing on this buoy causes it to leave a wake.

## USING CURRENT

Depending on their direction, currents can either assist or hinder your progress. Always try to sail with the current if you can. This illustration shows two boats reaching at 5 knots with and against a 2-knot current. Dorothy uses the current to achieve a net speed of 7 knots (5 + 2) over the ground that more than doubles Cynthia's net speed of 3 knots (5 - 2).

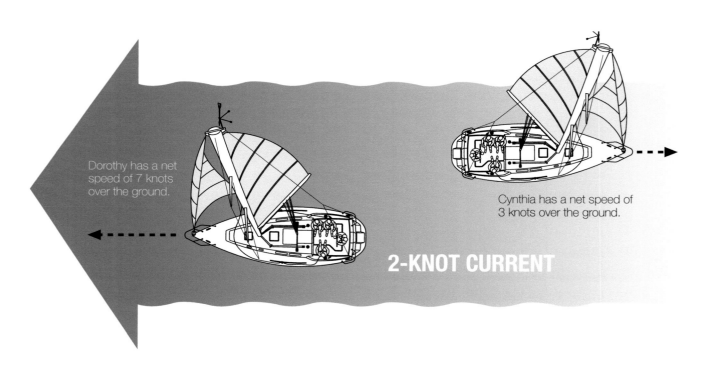

Dorothy has a net speed of 7 knots over the ground.

Cynthia has a net speed of 3 knots over the ground.

2-KNOT CURRENT

# PLANNING THE DAY

Whether it's a supertanker setting out for the other side of the world or your boat sailing to an anchorage on the next island, the passage plan lies at the core of safe progress. If the tanker takes the wrong route across the Pacific, it can cost the owners dearly. If you do not take the time to look carefully at where you plan to go and how you plan to get there, you may find yourself somewhere unexpected or in trouble of some sort. A typical plan will have three sections: clearing out as you leave harbor; making the miles; and working safely in at the other end.

## TOOLS FOR PLANNING - CHARTS AND CRUISING GUIDES

### ELECTRONIC CHART

For reasons already stated in this chapter, using a small screen chart plotter as the primary tool for planning a passage is a bad idea. Once underway, however, the plotter will offer an excellent means of assessing progress and finding where you are if you lose the picture. When working up a plan for leaving the harbor, switch on the plotter, check various zoom levels for layering, and see how its vector chart shapes up to the reality of the paper chart and the cruising guide. Become acclimated with its looks and note any areas where interrogation may be necessary so, if you need it on the way out, there will be no surprises.

### PAPER CHART

The chart is the basis of any plan. If you are operating with a paper chart and GPS, it makes a lot of sense to plot a waypoint outside the harbor at what will be the point of departure for the main passage. That defines the end of the exit plan. The task is now to work from where you are anchored, or docked, to this position. Even if you have a chart plotter, study the paper chart to find the best way out. It gives the most realistic overview and may also have useful notes.

### CRUISING GUIDE

There are first-class cruising guides available for most popular charter areas. They feature plans drawn by sailors with a realistic perspective on what you need to know. Charts don't always do this; electronic ones certainly do not. Guides offer invaluable notes as well as aerial photos of harbors, anchorages, marinas and hazards. In short, they do more than half of the job for you when used properly.

# PLANNING THE DEPARTURE

## CLEARING THE HARBOR

If you have already sailed into a harbor, it's reasonable to assume you will have a fair idea of how to sail out again. All charters start from a port of some sort; however, and unless you were there last year, the chances are that it will be strange to you on Day #1.

Even if you think you know the way, the buoyage could have changed at any point in time. This happens quite a bit, so if you head out full of confidence, only to discover that things are not what you expected, a stress-free experience is dashed quite suddenly. Even if you sailed into an anchorage last night, things can look different going out than they do coming in, and there may be a number of options for leaving that weren't relevant yesterday. A plan is the answer.

## PILOTAGE NOTES

Because people's minds function in different ways, the physical form of a pilotage plan is a personal thing. Draw up some notes with topics such as courses, distances, and turning points if that works for you. If you prefer, there is no law against jotting down some courses and distances on the paper chart, as long as you insist on a #2 pencil so that you can erase them without ruining a good chart. When the way out is simple, perhaps from an open roadstead, it's fine to inspect the data sources mentioned before, then cruise straight out to the waypoint, perhaps keeping dead center on the headlands if that's what the chart advises.

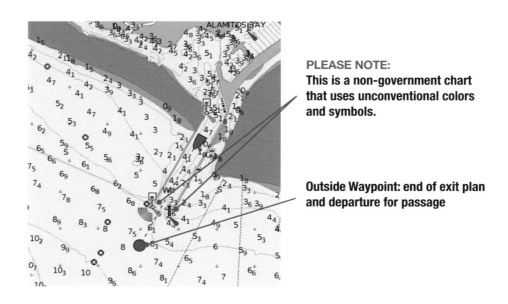

**PLEASE NOTE:**
**This is a non-government chart that uses unconventional colors and symbols.**

**Outside Waypoint: end of exit plan and departure for passage**

# PLANNING THE PASSAGE

## THE MAIN PASSAGE

Choose a passage chart that can accommodate your departure waypoint, as well as the new one you are going to plot, in a safe spot just outside the destination.

**Now, the main questions:**
- How far is it?
- What's the weather likely to be?
- Is there a reversing current involved, such as a tidal stream?

If the answers to these seem acceptable, you can move on to details.

**If so, when do you need to leave to be sure of a timely arrival?**
- Divide the number of miles by your probable speed in knots (modified for current, if any). Can you sail this passage in the time available?
- Qualify the route you plan to take for depth in general. If it includes bridges, check their overhead clearances.

## ESSENTIAL STRATEGY

Decide which route you may take and where you will make any major turns. Consider keeping under the lee of the land where possible, and maintaining a safe offing from any lee shores. Think again about the weather. You've decided about today, but what's likely to be served up for tomorrow?

## CRUISING GUIDES

Passage notes in a cruising guide can save a lot of time and trouble. A good cruising guide often has more information than just port plans and restaurant recommendations.

## TIDAL HEIGHTS

These will be unimportant in many venues, but where they do matter, it's best to work them out before you leave, rather than tackling the tables with the boat jumping around on a stiff beat.

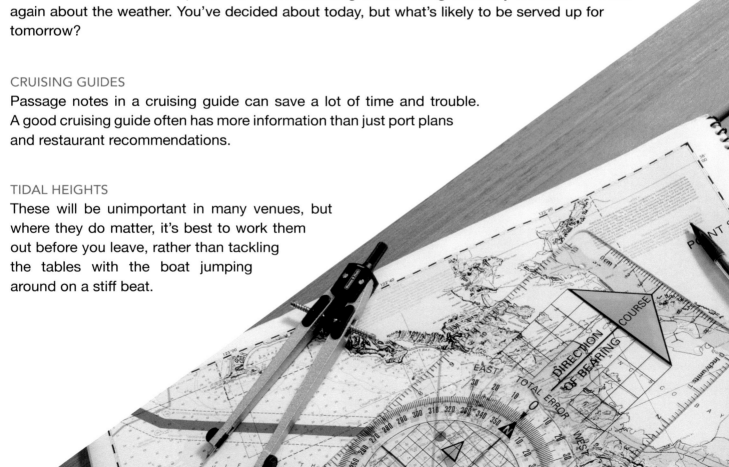

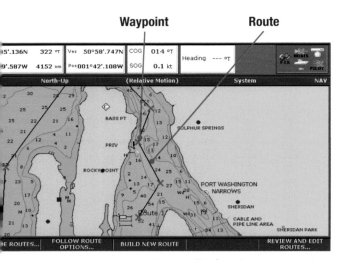

Waypoint          Route

Zoomed in for placing waypoints

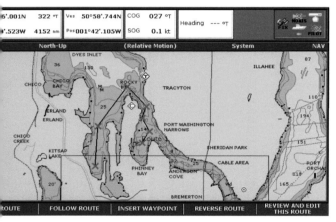

Zoomed out for overview of route

## CHECKING A WAYPOINT

1 Plot the charted waypoint and note its lat/long.

2 Punch the coordinates into the instrument.

3 With the boat still secured against the slip, press the *GoTo* button.

4 Note the range and bearing to the waypoint. Now plot these on the paper chart from the position of the boat.

5 No discrepancy? Good, the waypoint is proved.

6 Something wrong? Go back to the numbers and double-check for human error.

# WAYPOINTS AND ROUTES

A waypoint is a specific location that you enter into your chart plotter.

## WAYPOINTS

If the passage is anything other than a straight shot, you will be well served by plotting some waypoints. These can be placed at turning points and sited to avoid specific dangers. In waters with commercial activity, include shipping lanes under the heading of *Dangers*. If you turn up and there are no ships in sight, you can ignore the lanes; but where ships are plying their trade, it's generally best to stay well out of the way, even if you are technically the stand-on vessel.

A waypoint doesn't have to be somewhere you want to go. It can be equally effective marking an isolated danger you emphatically do not wish to visit. Navigating without a plotter, put a waypoint on a rock you want to avoid, hit the *GoTo* button, then ensure that the bearing changes steadily. Watch the range as well, and you should be fine.

Waypoint alarms can be helpful, especially where the waypoint is marking a danger rather than a safe place. Check the Settings in the GPS or plotter and arrange to be alerted at a range that suits the circumstances.

## CHECKING A WAYPOINT

A waypoint on a plotter screen is usually correct, because you will have set it by placing the cursor exactly where you want it, and then initiating some form of confirmation that you like what you see. On a paper chart, things may be different. Plot the waypoint and then read its lat/long. Then punch these coordinates into the GPS to set the waypoint. If a single digit comes adrift in the upper decimal range, you are a mile out. Even more dangerous is to be a hundred meters away in a world where pinpoint accuracy is expected. At the planning stage this can be avoided by using the steps to the left, because you generally know the precise position of the boat.

## ROUTES

A route in a GPS or plotter is a series of waypoints laced together electronically so that the boat can run from one to the next, following a preplanned track to her destination. As one is passed, the route switches automatically to the next, and so on. This works well for motorboats. Sailing craft, however, are prone to wander from the straight and narrow in search of a faster reach, to avoid a run, or just in order to lay something like their best course. By all means plot a route, but be aware that, if you are sailing, you may end up diverging from it.

## DISTANCE ON A CHART PLOTTER

Knowing how far you have to sail is a critical part of a passage plan. Chart plotters generally feature some sort of distance measuring device. Almost all plotters will read out the distance and bearing to the cursor from the ship, so you only need to hover the little cross over your destination to see how far it is.

Tidal current can have a big impact on distance in practice. A 30-mile run might seem a lot for some people's day sail, but if you can time it so there is a knot of fair current, suddenly, a six-knot boat has only 25 miles to make good. Get this wrong though, and there are 35 miles to go, which might be an hour too much.

## DIRECTION AND DISTANCE ON A PAPER CHART

To determine direction you will need a plotting tool which should come with the boat. There are a variety of plotting tools (e.g., parallel rulers, roller rulers, and protractors with one or two arms). All allow you to work in True or Magnetic. If you are strongly attached to a particular tool, bring it with you.

To measure distance on a paper chart, place one point of the dividers on the departure point and the other on the destination point. Move the dividers to the latitude scale on the side of the chart and read off how many minutes, or miles, you have to go.

**Distance is shown in the data box.**

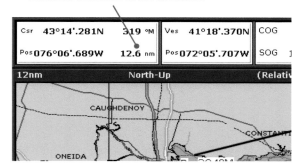

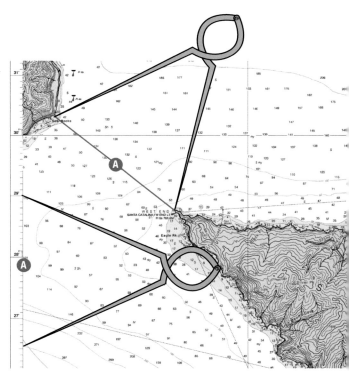

Use the latitude scale on the side of a paper chart to measure distance with dividers.

## TACKING

If you know you are going to be beating to the destination and have concerns about how wide your tacks should be, either for reasons of safety or just to tack efficiently down the rhumb line, set up a cross-track error rolling road screen to the relevant waypoint for a pictorial reference about the best moment to tack.

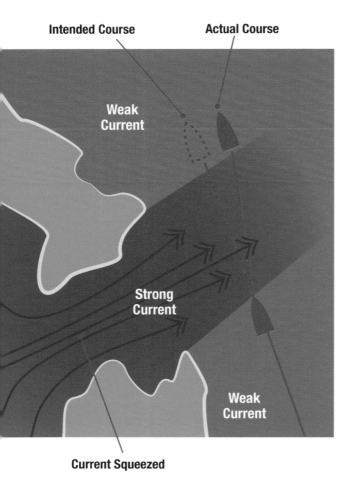

Intended Course    Actual Course

Weak Current

Strong Current

Weak Current

Current Squeezed

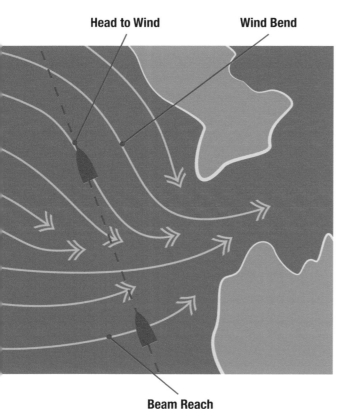

Head to Wind    Wind Bend

Beam Reach

## LONGER PASSAGES

Most charter companies place a limit on boats operating after dark. When the trip is a long one, special care is needed to ensure that you do not fall afoul of this. Inter-island passages in the Eastern Caribbean, for example, can take more time than anticipated. The seas can be heavy out of the lee of the land, and the current is squeezed between the islands and runs so hard to leeward that the skipper who expected to be sailing a beam reach ends up close-hauled and not even laying the course. Add to this the wind whipping round the end of an island and heading the boat, and you will see what can sometimes happen. Allow for a substantial contingency, ensure that there is fuel in the tank in case you have to motor sail, and start out early.

## PLANNING THE ARRIVAL

### ENTERING HARBOR

This is more or less a reverse of the procedure for leaving. As before, depending on the complexity or simplicity of the approach, you may decide on a plan beyond just driving in.

Study the chart in conjunction with cruising guides. Check how things look in these media against the chart plotter display so that there are no surprises if you use the plotter on the way in. Write a plan if it helps, noting critical factors such as buoy numeration, ranges that must not be missed, and dangers close to the route. Make notes on the chart if that suits you, but don't imagine that committing a complicated port entry with buoyed channels and ranges to memory will be enough; it won't be. Things can develop rapidly in harbors. The plotter will be a great comfort if you have one because, within the limits of its accuracy, it will always know where you are at any given time.

Make sure, therefore, that you have input the arrival waypoint as your starting position for entry, plus any others that might help you on the way up to the berth. Never forget that, however seductive it may appear, a plotter is an aid to navigation, not the final arbiter. That's you, and your own eyes are often the best instrument available.

# PROCEDURES UNDERWAY

## GETTING UNDERWAY

Once the anchor is up or the lines slipped, follow the exit plan, take your time, and be aware of the boat's position. The plotter will be a big help here, especially a tablet, but it's important not to become fascinated by the screen. There's a natural human tendency for this to happen and it can be fatal. The rocks lie under the water, not in amongst the hardware, so keep the lookout going and use your own eyes to gain a perspective. The plotter is there to help keep tabs on the boat's position, not to do the skipper's whole job.

When you are approaching the departure waypoint, you will probably be able to see the direction that the initial course is going to take you. Does it make sense? You wouldn't be the first to have plotted a reciprocal (180° out), or made some other simple error.

Now activate the next waypoint or set a course on the chart if there isn't one, and then trim the sails.

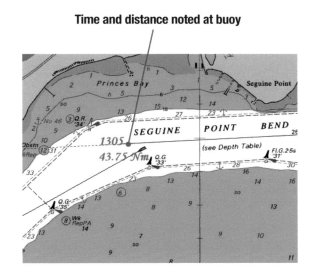

**Time and distance noted at buoy**

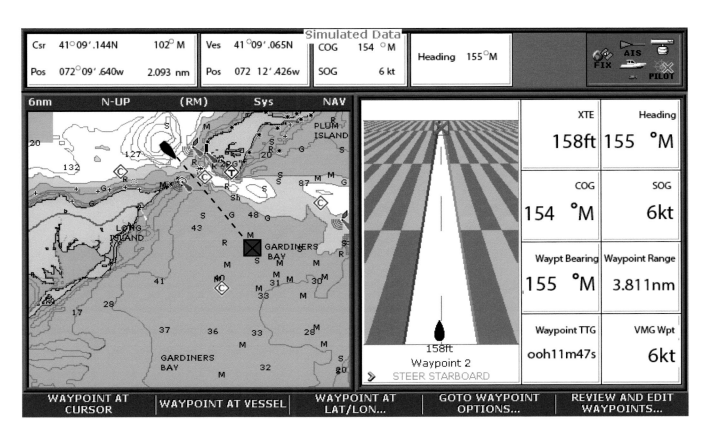

## ON PASSAGE

After confirming that the initial heading is sensible, log your departure. Along the route, monitor progress as you go with hourly or half-hourly log entries of your position, even if you choose not to plot this on the paper chart. Since you will almost certainly be within sight of land, maintain a visual perspective on progress. A good navigator will keep the rest of the crew briefed as to how things are going. Morale is kept up if people know how long it is likely to be before they can grab their snorkels or pour themselves a drink. As waypoints approach, be ready for any course change that may follow, then select the next one or the destination waypoint as appropriate.

Note columns for time, log, course, weather and remarks in your log. Engine hours can also be useful. Some authorities believe there should be a column for latitude/longitude position if the yacht is equipped with electronics. Put one in if it makes you feel comfortable.

## UNDERWAY PROCEDURES

### SHIP'S LOG BOOK

Before GPS, nobody doubted the importance of maintaining the ship's log book, at minimum on an hourly basis. Entries in the log, especially the positions, times, distance log readings and courses, provided all that was needed to work up an estimated position at any moment. Now that GPS gives a constantly updated, accurate position, it's easy to forget about the log book altogether. This can be a very bad mistake, as navigation screens do go blank from time to time. For confirmation of why, go to Page 116 and read about what happens when the navigation screens go blank.

Some charter boats come with a log book already printed in columns with spaces for comments. If yours doesn't, bring an exercise book — a good plan anyway. Open it at a double-page spread.

Rule columns on one page and keep the other clear for comments. The minimum information that should be recorded are Time, Course Steered, and the Distance Log Reading. This data will allow you to determine your approximate position independently from any electronics. Other columns in the logbook might include Position, Speed Over Ground (SOG) and Course Over Ground (COG) from GPS, Weather/Sea Conditions, and the Barometer Reading. It takes only a minute to make these entries every hour or half-hour as appropriate. They provide a record should any serious mishap occur, and without them you are literally lost if GPS fails when you are beyond immediate eyeball confirmation of your position.

## PROACTIVE NOT REACTIVE

In part, the seaman is always anticipating and the crew are also looking out to keep ahead of the game with the piloting. Also, by foreseeing trouble, he or she can make sure it doesn't happen. The voyage proceeds without incident, but only because the skipper is on the ball.

Look to see what's coming before it arrives. In other words, be a proactive skipper, always one step ahead; not a reactive one who spends too much time trying to rectify situations that need never have happened.

## AVOIDING COLLISION

### THE STEADY BEARING AT SEA

The big secret to staying clear of collisions with other boats or objects is, that by the basic rules of geometry, any object, whether fixed or afloat and whose range is closing and is on a steady bearing, is going to hit you or you are going to hit it. If the object in question is a ship out at sea with nothing visible behind it but the horizon, the surest way to visually check its bearing is to observe it over a hand-bearing compass. If it bears 125M now and still does ten minutes later, there is going to be a close-quarters situation in due course.

You can also check a steady bearing by sitting in one place — perhaps behind the wheel — and not moving your head more than a few inches for several minutes. Note the bearing of the ship over something on board such as a stanchion. If it stays the same, watch out!

### A STEADY BEARING NEAR LAND

An easier way of confirming a steady bearing is to line up the object (e.g., ship, rock, buoy) against its background. If it is coinciding with, for example, a church spire or the corner of a field, a range (sometimes called a transit), has been established. This means that if the range is closing you are going to hit it, or it's going to hit you. Race boats use this method all the time. It only stops working if the object is very close to its background in comparison with its distance from you.

Old hands use these methods all the time, often subliminally. Less experienced sailors must remind themselves to do it. Everything on the water is sliding sideways to some extent. The boat may well not be going where she's pointing. These simple ways of determining drift and closing situations are the very essence of seamanship.

**Official Range**

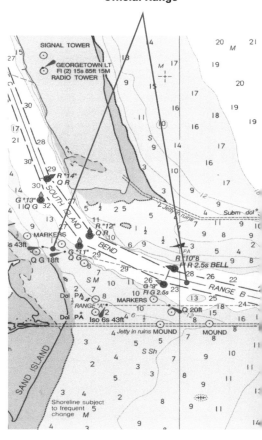

By lining up the two markers of this "official" range, you will be able to stay in the middle of the channel.

111

# KEEPING ON TRACK

At the planning stage, you will have put in some effort to define a safe track to your destination. Once under way, current, leeway and even inattentive steering can nibble away at this until the boat is nowhere near the line you have decided to follow on the chart. There are four main ways of avoiding this:

## COMPASS BEARING

If you do not have a chart plotter or GPS, take a bearing on the destination as you leave your departure point. Steer to keep this constant. If it changes, it is no longer on a steady bearing so you aren't going to hit it which, in this case, is what you actually want to happen. You are using the collision avoidance system in reverse and it works perfectly.

## NATURAL RANGE

This is the best method of all, including the electronic ones laid out below. If possible, always line up two objects behind where you are going. If the destination is a pier head or some other definable object, so much the better. Use that and a suitable item behind it. The objects can be anything at all, even a cow in a field so long as it doesn't get up and walk around. Once locked onto this range, the boat cannot deviate more than a few yards from her desired track.

If the destination is too far off to observe by eye, keep aware of the general background and use natural ranges to watch for sideways movement. Training the eye to do this is the seaman's best weapon in the battle to keep on the straight and narrow.

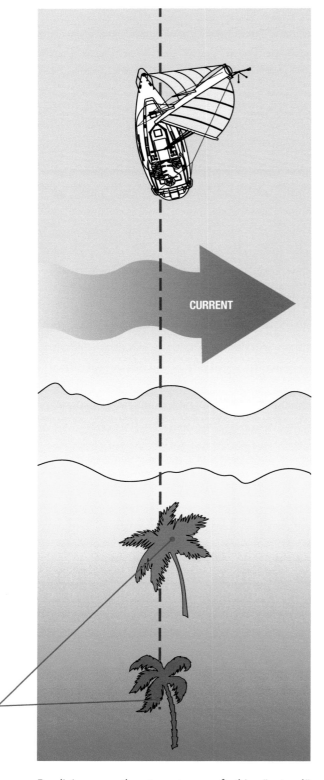

By lining up the two trees of this "natural" range, you will be able to see if you are being set off course.

## DISTANCE AND BEARING

Using GPS with a paper chart, be sure to have a destination waypoint activated by pressing the *GoTo* button when you leave the previous waypoint behind. The GPS will now read out distance and bearing. Distance is useful, but bearing is critical. Steer so as to keep this number constant and you are right on track.

## PROJECTED TRACK

This is where the chart plotter really delivers its magic. Search the menus for the vectors and activate the projected track line. Do not confuse this with heading, which is merely the way you are steering at any moment; we know well that a boat is often not going where she is pointing. Projected track shows where you will actually end up and what your track will cross on the way, which is much more useful. If you have deviated from the desired track, you can see at a glance whether the new track crosses any dangers and thereby adjust accordingly.

What might surprise you is how many sailors never use this most important feature of the chart plotter. As long as there is no datum shift and you have drilled down through the layers on the chart to see what's really there, it will keep you safe even when you can't see where you are going.

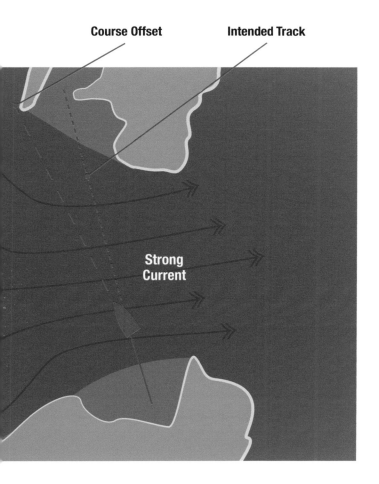

Course Offset    Intended Track

Strong
Current

## REMAINING ON YOUR INTENDED TRACK

A prudent skipper, aware that the water itself may be moving and carrying the boat with it, needs to take appropriate action. You have been offset from your intended track if: your departure point is no longer directly astern; a fix does not place you on your intended track; or the course to your destination is changing. You will need to make an adjustment to your heading in order to compensate for this offset.

If working on a paper chart, check your position by taking bearings on nearby fixed objects. The objects should be as near to right angles as possible. Plot the bearing lines on the chart. Where they cross should be near your position. A depth sounder can be used to complete or confirm a fix.

## FOG AND POOR VISIBILITY

When you see fog developing, your first action is to fix your position. Even if you have electronics, this may be the last chance you will have to reassure yourself that the device is functioning as it should.

### SAFETY ACTIONS TO BE TAKEN

- ▶ Increase the lookouts to include forward and amidships.
- ▶ Hoist the radar reflector.
- ▶ Listen hard for sound signals and other vessels.
- ▶ Set a radar watch if appropriate.
- ▶ Ensure that everyone on board is wearing a life jacket in case of collision.
- ▶ Sound fog signal.

### Sound Signals for Vessels in Restricted Visibility:

▬▬▬ One prolonged blast every two minutes indicates a vessel under power.

▬▬▬ ● ● One prolonged blast followed by two short blasts every two minutes indicates a vessel under sail. Be aware that other vessels will also sound this signal (e.g., vessels engaged in towing, fishing, pushing, and vessels restricted in their ability to maneuver).

## PLAYING IT SAFE

If you cannot make it to a safe harbor and there is heavy traffic around, you have two options: either sail far out to sea and heave-to; or, preferably, make for shoal waters inshore and anchor in an area shallow enough that a commercial ship cannot hit you.

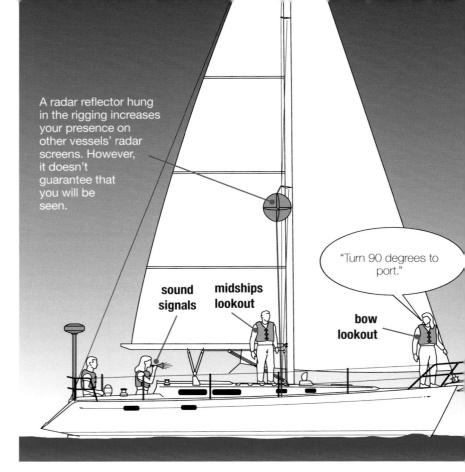

A radar reflector hung in the rigging increases your presence on other vessels' radar screens. However, it doesn't guarantee that you will be seen.

"Turn 90 degrees to port."

sound signals

midships lookout

bow lookout

Some objects such as smaller fiberglass vessels will only show a radar return at close range. Change the range setting frequently.

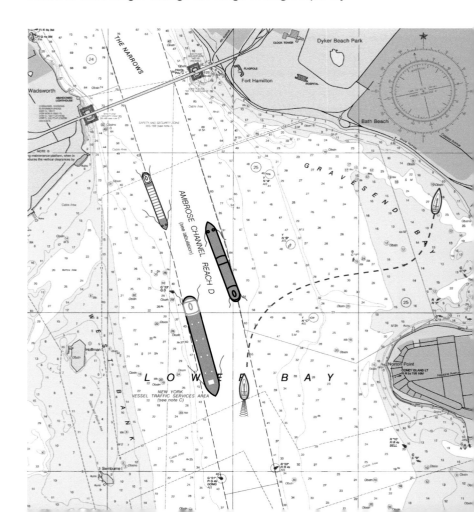

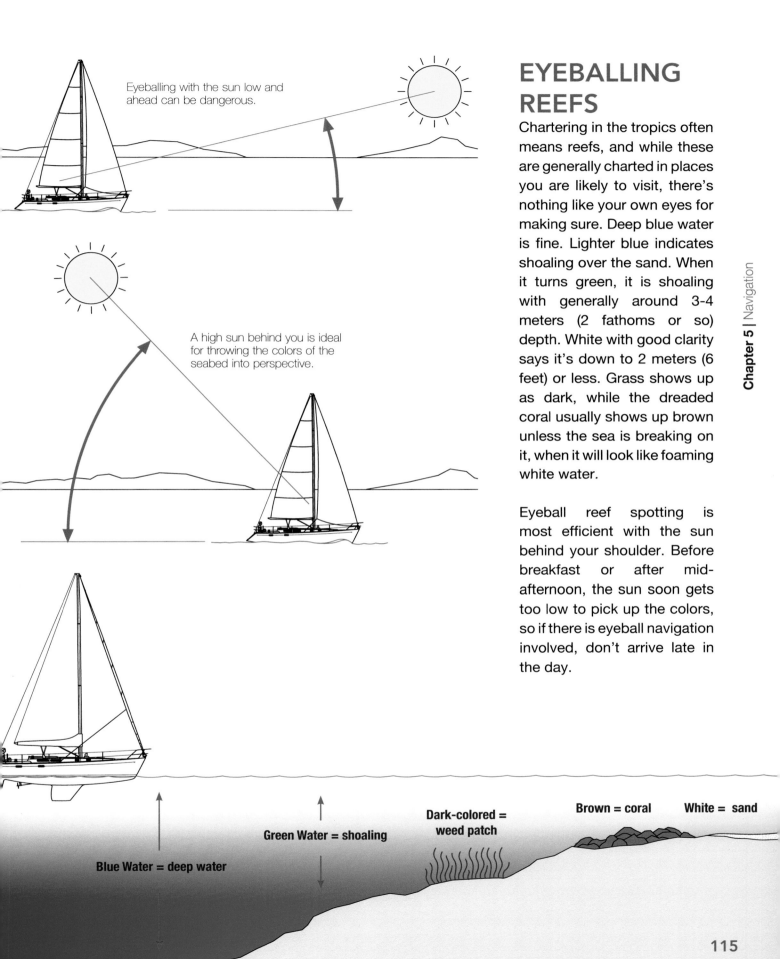

Eyeballing with the sun low and ahead can be dangerous.

A high sun behind you is ideal for throwing the colors of the seabed into perspective.

# EYEBALLING REEFS

Chartering in the tropics often means reefs, and while these are generally charted in places you are likely to visit, there's nothing like your own eyes for making sure. Deep blue water is fine. Lighter blue indicates shoaling over the sand. When it turns green, it is shoaling with generally around 3-4 meters (2 fathoms or so) depth. White with good clarity says it's down to 2 meters (6 feet) or less. Grass shows up as dark, while the dreaded coral usually shows up brown unless the sea is breaking on it, when it will look like foaming white water.

Eyeball reef spotting is most efficient with the sun behind your shoulder. Before breakfast or after mid-afternoon, the sun soon gets too low to pick up the colors, so if there is eyeball navigation involved, don't arrive late in the day.

Blue Water = deep water

Green Water = shoaling

Dark-colored = weed patch

Brown = coral

White = sand

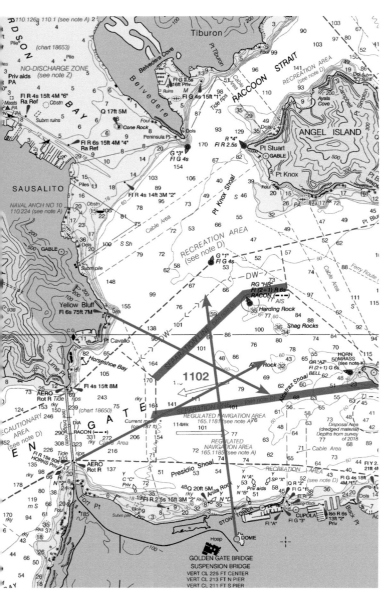

Take a bearing on a charted object that you can see and positively identify. Plot that line on the chart. This is known as a Line of Position (LOP); you are somewhere along this line. Plot LOPs from two other objects. The center of the triangle formed by the intersection of these three lines is your position. This is called a fix. Label it with the time.

# IF THE SCREENS GO BLANK

Everyone navigating with electronics suffers a truly upsetting feeling when the screens go blank. It may be a system failure on board or a problem with the signal. For whatever reason, the GPS and/or the chart plotter has shut down and you are left with no electronic fix, no projected track, and no waypoints. If there are any backup systems (such as navigation apps on your phone or a crew member's tablet), activate them. In addition, take a deep breath, look around, and reorient yourself. This is no more than an inconvenience. As long as you have a good paper chart, plotting tools, a compass, and have been keeping track of your position, you will be able to carry on safely.

If the visibility is good and you can confirm your position by eye and reconcile it with the chart, keep going on the course you have been sailing.

If you are unsure of your position, you will need to plot a fix. Confirm your position with the depth sounder. From the fix, plot the course to the next point where you will change course or to your destination.

Examine the chart along and near the course line for hazards and landmarks. As long as there are no hazards along your course line, continue with the plan. If there are, modify the course to give any potential problems a very wide berth. Using ranges either ahead or astern will allow you to proceed with confidence.

Watch for any additional clues to confirm or deny how the plan is working. Monitor the depth sounder to make sure it matches where you expect to be on the chart. If not, slow down or stop, recheck your position, make a new plan, and move on.

## RUNNING A CONTOUR

By deliberately steering wide to the upwind or upcurrent side of the entrance, you will know with confidence which way to turn when you reach your chosen depth. Keep the depth constant by working in and out across the contour line until you locate the channel mark. Once at the mark, you can turn into the channel and steer down the right-hand edge, keeping an eye on the depth sounder to confirm your location along the edge of the channel.

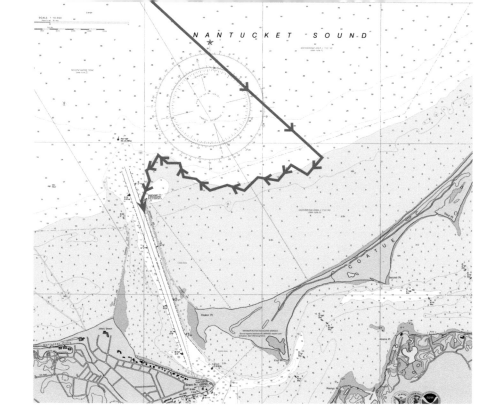

## COMING IN

When you reach the harbor mouth, the outer boats in the anchorage, or the destination waypoint, stay alert; the passage is not yet over. Many boats suffer incidents at the end of the day because the skipper relaxed too early. There are still decisions to be made and questions to be answered: "Where can I anchor? Will there be room for me in the marina? Are there moorings available or can I tie to the town quay?" The cruising guide can often help. Some marinas keep a listening watch on the VHF radio (see the cruising guide for channels). A cell phone will solve many issues. Enter slowly and have a look around. When unsure, tie up at a likely looking berth, and seek out the authorities.

Regardless of your choice, there are procedures to be followed. In the Caribbean, simply sailing from one island to the next can result in crossing an international border. This means that you will need to deal with Customs and Immigration. Even when sailing from one island to another in the Greek Islands, you will need to check in with the local authorities and follow their instructions. Additionally, there are often charges for such things as berthing, entry to national parks, or just fees for cruising their waters.

And finally, don't forget to make dinner reservations!

117

Chapter 6

# HEALTH, SAFETY AND EMERGENCY

Despite the interconnectedness of the modern world, there may be times when assistance is miles or hours away. A prudent skipper will be ready to react quickly and properly to such things as an injured crew member, an equipment failure, or an overboard situation.

## HYPOTHERMIA, SEASICKNESS AND HEAT EMERGENCIES

Sailing can expose you to extreme conditions, both hot and cold. On hot, windless days, you will be exposed to a lot of sun. On windy, overcast days, the cool spray coming over the bow can send a chill down your spine. Be prepared for these changes. Drink a lot of water and wear clothing that protects your skin and head from the sun. Have warm clothing along in case the weather turns foul. Put your pants or jacket on before you get cold. Additionally, you should know the warning signals for heat and cold emergencies and what to do in those situations.

## HYPOTHERMIA

### SIGNALS

- Shivering
- Impaired judgment
- Dizziness
- Numbness
- Change in level of consciousness
- Weakness
- Glassy stare; physical symptoms may vary because age, body size and clothing will cause individual differences.

### TREATMENT

Medical assistance should be given to anyone with hypothermia. Until medical assistance arrives, these steps should be taken:

- Check breathing and pulse.
- Move the person to a warm place.
- Remove all wet clothing. Gradually warm the person by wrapping the individual in blankets or putting on dry clothes. Do not warm a person too quickly, such as immersing in warm water. Rapid rewarming may cause dangerous heart rhythms. Hot water bottles and chemical heat packs may be used if first wrapped in a towel or blanket before applying.
- Give warm, nonalcoholic and noncaffeinated liquids to a conscious person only.

## HEAT EXHAUSTION

### SIGNALS

- Cool, moist, pale skin
- Heavy sweating
- Headache
- Dizziness
- Nausea
- Weakness, exhaustion

### TREATMENT

Without prompt care, heat exhaustion can advance to a more serious condition — heat stroke. First aid includes:

- Move the person to a cool environment.
- Remove clothing soaked with perspiration and loosen any tight clothing.
- Apply cool, wet towels or sheets.
- Fan the person.
- Give the person a half glass (4 oz.) of cool water every 15 minutes.

## HEAT STROKE

### SIGNALS

- Red, hot, dry or moist skin
- Very high temperature
- Changes in level of consciousness
- Vomiting
- Rapid, weak pulse
- Rapid, shallow breathing

### TREATMENT

Heat stroke is life threatening. Anyone suffering from heat stroke needs to be cooled and an EMS technician should be contacted immediately. To care for heat stroke:

- Move the person to a cool environment.
- Apply cool, wet towels or sheets.
- If available, place ice or cold packs on the person's wrists and ankles, groin, each armpit and neck.
- If unconscious, check breathing and pulse.

## SEASICKNESS

**Sailing can cause motion sickness. You can reduce your chances of becoming seasick by getting plenty of sleep the night before you go sailing.**

- Eat before going out, but avoid greasy, heavy foods and alcohol.
- Dress warmly.
- Some people use wrist bands that activate accupressure points. Others rely on prescription medications such as Scopolamine.
- Symptoms include yawning, burping, paleness, a headache or nausea. Get on deck for fresh air and watch the horizon to calm your sensory system or, steer the boat. Eating salted crackers or drinking a carbonated cola might help. In really bad cases, lie on your back in a spot where you are sheltered from cold and spray.

### NOTE:
US Sailing recommends you attend first aid and CPR classes, both of which are available nationwide.

# TREATING ROPE, STOVE AND SUN BURNS

If a crew member sustains a burn that doesn't break the skin, cover the wound with a cool, damp cloth to soothe and reduce the pain. Follow the same procedure for a burn that breaks the skin, but seek medical assistance immediately. Keep the person quiet and comfortable. Do not apply grease, oil or gooey substances to the affected area and do not attempt to break the blisters.

## TIPS

- Disclose health issues such as medical problems, medications, allergic reactions or pregnancy in advance to the captain and, if willing, others on board.
- Check out the first aid kit before leaving the charter dock.

## HEALTH SMART

If you are allergic to bee stings, you are likely to be allergic to jellyfish stings. Consult your physician before setting sail.

## EMERGENCY PROCEDURES

Even in very popular charter areas, help can be several hours away. It's prudent for someone aboard to be trained in CPR and first aid.

- In the event of a life-threatening accident, immediately summon help on the VHF radio with a Mayday call, a cell phone to call the charter company, or any other means of getting attention or assistance.
- Ensure that the person has an open airway. If there are no signs of breathing, start CPR immediately and continue until help arrives.
- Control severe bleeding with direct pressure to the wound.
- For treatment of shock, elevate the person's feet, loosen restrictive clothing, and keep them cool and calm.
- Move them as little as possible, particularly if they have fallen, and get assistance as soon as possible.

## FIRST AID CHECKLIST

**FOOD POISONING** - Contaminated, improperly cooked or stored meat, fish and poultry, as well as unwashed fruits and vegetables, can cause violent cramps, nausea, vomiting and diarrhea. Seek professional assistance. With severe vomiting, don't force food or liquids. As soon as practical, have the person take small amounts of water, rehydration drinks or other nonalcoholic liquids. The person should rest quietly for 24 hours, consuming only liquids and small quantities of soft food such as salted crackers or boiled rice. Severe or prolonged diarrhea or vomiting causes dehydration and requires professional treatment. Ask your charter company about freshly caught seafood and fish that may be poisonous.

**DIARRHEA** - Unfamiliar foods and situations can cause diarrhea. Prevent dehydration by drinking water, rehydration drinks or other nonalcoholic liquids. Avoid activity and stay out of the sun. If diarrhea persists, get medical assistance.

**DEHYDRATION** - Drink plenty of water and other nonalcoholic liquids to help your system adjust to warmer climates. Stay out of the sun as much as possible.

## COMMON INJURIES IN THE WATER

- Clean all coral cuts with diluted hydrogen peroxide (50% water and 50% hydrogen peroxide) and treat immediately with antibiotic cream. Beware of infection. If the cut becomes red, continue with the antibiotic cream. Reduce swelling with ice. Seek medical assistance if healing doesn't occur or red streaking appears around the wound.
- If a crew member steps on a sea urchin, apply mild acid such as vinegar or lemon juice, and seek medical attention.
- If a crew member steps on a stingray, put their foot in a bucket of the hottest tolerable water until the pain subsides. Medical attention is needed to clean the puncture wound and remove any parts of the stinger.

# OVERBOARD RESCUE

A well-rounded skipper has the experience and practice to choose the method that will offer the best chance of success based on the boat and circumstances. By its very nature, rescuing a person in the water (PIW) is always a surprise. Managing this situation is a multi-step process: return the boat to the PIW; stop alongside; attach the person to the boat; and bring the person aboard. Any injuries, shock, or hypothermia must be treated. Cool heads, quick reactions, and a practiced response are required. It cannot be over emphasized: the key to a safe, prompt, overboard rescue is **Practice! Practice! Practice!**

## RETURNING TO THE PIW

Many methods of returning a boat to a PIW have been devised and they all have the same goals: keep everyone safe; stay close to the PIW; maintain visual contact; return quickly; and stop the boat alongside the PIW. Several of the most widely accepted methods will be outlined below. Practice each of these methods in a variety of conditions to determine which is best for your boat and sailing conditions, and to ensure that your response will be automatic. There is a series of first steps that need to be done immediately and are common to all rescue methods.

1. Whoever sees the person fall overboard should loudly shout, **"CREW OVERBOARD!"** This shout will alert everyone on board of the situation.
2. Designate a spotter by name. That person's only job is to keep their eyes on and point at the PIW. If short-handed, this job may fall to the helmsman.
3. Toss the throwable floating device into the water as close to the PIW as possible. This provides flotation for the PIW (or additional flotation if the PIW is already wearing a life jacket), and its bright color is easy for the spotter to see.
4. Activate the "Overboard Button" on the GPS, which may require several steps.
5. Consider issuing a **"MAYDAY"** immediately or very soon.

Practicing overboard rescue with safety equipment provided will help get the PIW back to the boat promptly.

## USING THE ENGINE DURING A RESCUE

All of the following rescue methods should be practiced and mastered under sail power alone. However, all of them call for the engine to be started. There can be situations where even a short use of the engine can make the difference between success and having to make another attempt. This is particularly true when controlling the boat's speed during the final approach, where a small miscalculation can easily be corrected with the use of the engine.

# FIGURE-8 RESCUE METHOD

The Figure-8 is the most universal method. It will work with big and small boats, in heavy and light air, from any point of sail, and with many or few crew left on board. It also does not involve jibing.

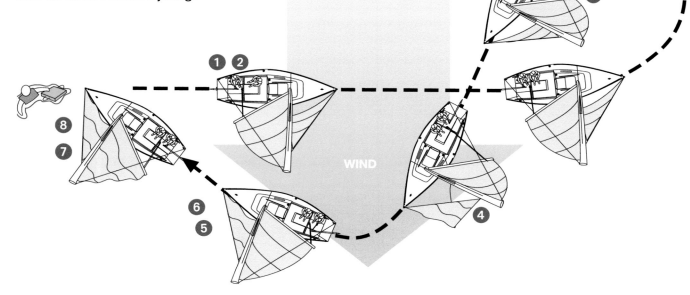

❶ Immediately steer the boat to a beam reach and trim the main appropriately. Check for lines in the water, start the engine and leave it in neutral.

❷ Sail approximately four boat lengths away.

❸ Tack directly from the beam reach to a deep broad reach. Allow the jib to backwind, as it will help direct the bow downwind to the deep broad reach. As you finish the tack, sheet the main out all the way.

❹ Once on the deep broad reach, release the jib completely.

❺ Turn upwind and approach the PIW on a close reach. If you have turned towards the PIW too early, the main cannot luff completely and you need to quickly turn downwind again.

❻ Repeat Step #5 until the approach course is a close reach and the main is luffing completely.

❼ Aim the bow of the boat six or seven feet upwind of the PIW. Control boat speed with the main.

❽ Turn off the engine when the PIW is between the bow and the shrouds. Stop the boat with the PIW alongside to leeward.

**NOTE:** You want to be on a close reach when you return to the PIW. When in doubt, point the boat at the PIW, assess your point of sail and adjust. When upwind, bear away a boat length or two and test again. When downwind, use the engine or begin the maneuver again.

# QUICK-STOP RESCUE METHOD

The Quick-Stop Method is particularly useful if you are sailing close-hauled or nearly so when the person falls overboard. From other points of sail, the geometry is altered and the sail handling more complex. This method involves a jibe and, in smaller boats in heavy air with the main sheeted in, that may be difficult or impossible.

❶ Maintain the close-hauled course for two or three boat lengths.

❷ Turn the boat slowly into and through the No-Go Zone until the PIW is on your beam to leeward. Check for lines in the water, start the engine and leave it in neutral.

❸ Slowly bear away, keeping the PIW on your beam and two to three boat lengths away. Do not allow the boat to spiral inward toward the PIW.

❹ When the jib jibes, release it.

❺ When the main jibes, release it.

❻ Turn upwind and approach the PIW on a close reach, aiming the bow of the boat six or seven feet upwind of the PIW. Control the boat speed with the main.

❼ Turn off the engine when the PIW is between the bow and the shrouds. Stop the boat with the PIW alongside to leeward.

**NOTE:** Do not spiral inward toward the PIW as you bear away. The boat needs some distance to stop. Release each sail as it jibes. If you don't, the boat will accelerate as you head up toward the PIW.

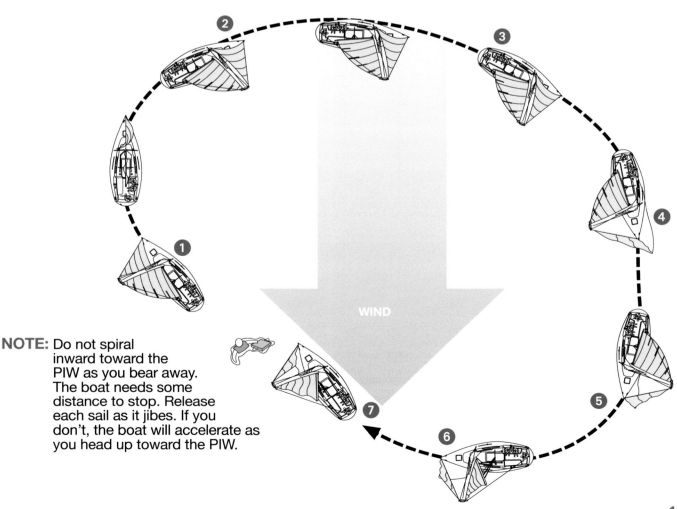

WIND

## BUTTONHOOK RETURN METHOD

This method is a modification of the rescue sling-type rescue and reduces the time it takes to make contact with the PIW. As with all rescue sling methods, it requires the active participation of the PIW and will not work if the PIW is unconscious, seriously injured or hypothermic. It has the advantage of returning to and attaching the PIW concurrently.

1. Immediately come to a close reach and deploy the rescue sling. Check for lines in the water, start the engine and leave it in neutral.

2. Check to ensure complete deployment of the rescue sling.

3. Tack to a deep broad reach, taking care not to run over the trailing sling line.

4. Approach with the PIW on your windward side.

5. Head up to a close reach as you pass the PIW.

6. Ease the sheets to slow and stop the boat when the rescue line comes within reach of the PIW.

7. Drop or furl the sails when the PIW is in the sling. Turn off the engine. Pull or winch the PIW alongside.

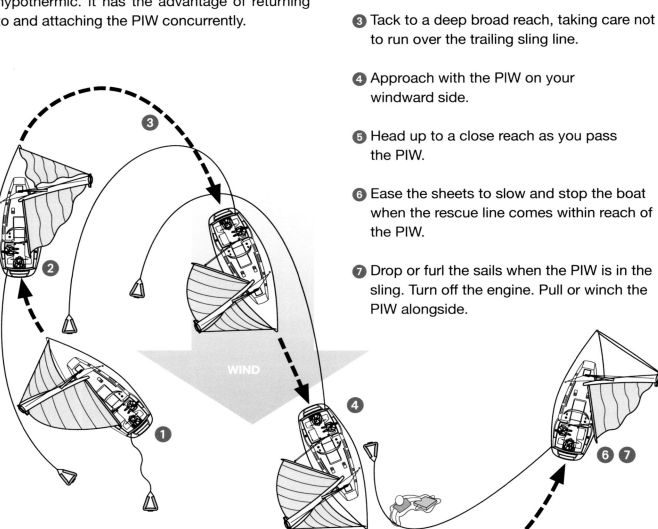

A rescue sling is a floating device attached to the boat by a length of floating line that doubles as a hoisting sling to retrieve a PIW from the water.

**NOTE:** If you stop too soon after rounding up, the line may not be within reach of the PIW. Use your engine to move the boat and the line upwind toward the PIW or pull some of the line into the boat and within reach of the PIW.

# OVERBOARD RESCUE IN CATAMARANS

Because of a catamaran's higher speed and upwind sailing characteristics, the Quick-Stop and Figure-8 Rescue Methods may be more difficult to perform than with a monohull. It is advisable to immediately start the engines to enhance maneuverability.

In the **Figure-8 Rescue Method**, it may be necessary to use the engines to complete the tack. After tacking, avoid going too far downwind, as cruising catamarans make considerable leeway at slow speeds and do not point as high as monohulls.

In the **Quick-Stop Rescue Method**, engine assistance may be necessary to complete the tack and again as you bear away to jibe because the mainsail remains tightly sheeted in.

## NOTES:
▶ If the catamaran is sailing at a speed with the wind well aft, motoring back may be the only workable solution.
▶ Because of a catamaran's high freeboard, the stern steps may be the only place possible to reach a PIW.

## HEAVE-TO RESCUE METHOD

This is an alternative method well suited to catamarans. Immediately start both engines and heave-to upwind of the PIW. Then use the engines to control your position and angle to the wind as you drift down to the PIW.

❶ Start the engines.

❷ Heave-to using engines as necessary.

❸ Use forward and reverse as necessary to control your drift to the PIW.

❹ Once the PIW is alongside, turn off the engines.

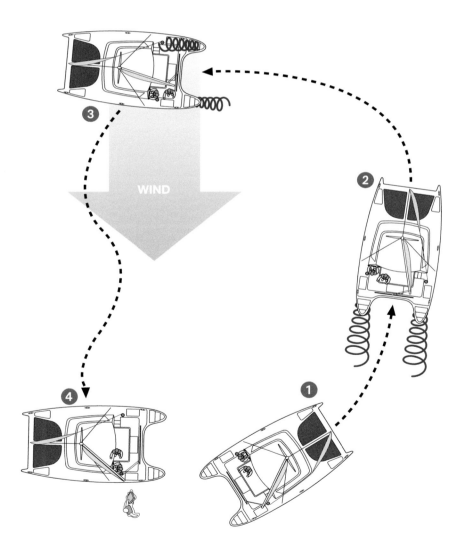

WIND

## RETURN WHILE UNDER POWER

When motoring either a catamaran or a monohull, the process of returning to the PIW is simpler. There are no sails with which to be concerned and it is just a matter of positioning the boat properly for the final approach.

❶ Hold course until the PIW is clear of the prop.

❷ Then turn downwind and position the boat so that the PIW is approximately three or four boat lengths away and the course back would be a close reach if sailing.

❸ Slow down and turn toward the PIW.

❹ Make your final approach on this course, aiming the bow six or seven feet upwind of the PIW.

❺ Turn off the engine when the PIW is between the bow and the shrouds. Stop the boat with the PIW alongside to leeward.

WIND

**NOTE:** Use the engine to control the speed of the final approach.

# RESCUING A PERSON

## ATTACHING THE PIW

Unless the rescue has been made with a sling and properly secured to a cleat, secure the PIW to the boat. The only exception to this would be if the PIW can be pulled aboard immediately after stopping the boat alongside, which is unlikely on high freeboard boats.

**Lack of attachment is often the weak link in overboard rescues.**

If the PIW can assist in their rescue, a heaving line can be used, but PIWs have been known to let a line slip out of their grasp as they succumb to fatigue and hypothermia. You may have to clip a line to the PIW's harness or slip a bowline under their arms and around their chest. Once the PIW is attached to the boat, there will be time to take the steps necessary to bring them aboard without fear of losing contact and having to start the rescue all over again. Assign a crew member to monitor the condition of the PIW while preparations are made.

## GETTING THE PIW ABOARD

Getting the PIW aboard may be the most difficult part of the entire rescue process. The freeboard on most modern sailboats is too high to be scaled unaided and the PIW will need some form of assistance. Lifelines increase this distance. How to lift the PIW aboard will depend upon many things, including whether the PIW is injured or can help with the process, how many people are on board, and what devices are available.

If the PIW is unable to help with the rescue, it may be necessary to put a rescue swimmer (wearing a life jacket and attached to the boat with a safety line) into the water to assist the PIW.

### BOARDING LADDER

It may be possible for the PIW to climb back aboard via a boarding ladder with, or even without, assistance. On most modern boats, however, the ladder is mounted at the stern and it may be dangerous to approach if it thrashes up and down as the boat hobby-horses in a seaway. A ladder that mounts amidships may be much safer.

### THE DINGHY

If you are towing a dinghy, it may be much easier for the PIW to board this. If necessary, a crew member can get into the dinghy and assist.

### THE LOOP

Hang a line over the side with a bowline tied in its end with the loop one or two feet below the surface of the water. This provides a step for the PIW, and the PIW can use the line to help keep themselves vertical and not allow their feet to go under the boat.

NOTE: The loop shown in the photo to the left is using a lazy halyard that can be winched up.

Chapter 6 | Health, Safety and Emergency

Chapter 6 | Health, Safety and Emergency

127

## THE ELEVATOR

This is a line with one end made fast to the boat and the other led to a winch. The slack in between is placed in the water and the PIW stands on it. The line is then winched in, slowly lifting the PIW until the PIW can climb aboard. It is often very useful to have a line around the PIW's chest to help them remain upright.

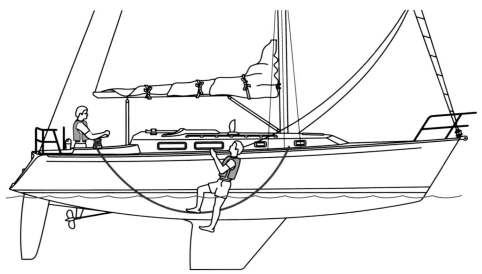

## RESCUE SLING WITH BLOCK AND TACKLE

If a sling was used, the PIW is already attached to the boat and ready to be hoisted aboard. Rig a block and tackle between the end of a halyard and the PIW, lead the tail to a winch, and haul the PIW aboard. Lacking a block and tackle system, attach the halyard directly to the rescue sling. It is useful to have a crew member ready to assist the PIW. Unfortunately, this may well involve lifting the PIW vertically by the shoulders. Try to raise the legs as soon as you can.

# AFTERCARE

Take the greatest care of the PIW, as they often succumb to hypothermia (refer to *Safety at Sea: A Guide to Safety Under Sail and Personal Survival* for further information on prevention, symptoms and treatment). Warm them gently with sleeping bags if cold, keep them lying down if the affair has been at all traumatic, and generally treat them like shock cases. If you have any doubts regarding treatment or there is any suspicion of internal injuries, shock. or water in the lungs, call up a "PAN-PAN medico" and ask for advice.

# UNFOULING A PROPELLER

If your engine dies suddenly with no obvious reason, shift to neutral and restart it. If the engine runs in neutral but dies again as soon as it is put in gear, suspect a fouled prop. Your lookout may not have seen the float from a crab trap or perhaps one of your lines was accidentally trailing over the side. In any case, the engine is unavailable until the fouled prop is cleared.

If you are in calm conditions, you may be able to free the prop while standing on the swim ladder using a boat hook. It may help to rotate the propeller shaft by hand in the opposite direction in which it fouled. If conditions make this unsafe, sail the boat to a safe location and anchor before attempting to free the prop. If you are in danger of drifting onto a lee shore, anchor immediately.

If you snagged a trap, try to pull the line to the surface with the boat hook, buoy it with a fender (so the fisherman can retrieve it), cut it loose, and then free the prop.

As a last resort, you may have to put someone in the water. Do this only in calm conditions and attach the swimmer to the boat with a safety line. The fouled line can be cut away with a sharp knife or hacksaw. Do not restart the engine until the swimmer is back on board. If unable to anchor or sail, call for assistance.

## Dos and Don'ts

▶ Do shift into neutral as soon as you detect a fouled propeller.
▶ Don't shift into reverse to attempt to free the line.
▶ Do shut down the engine while attempting to unfoul the propeller.
▶ Do ensure there is no load on the line while unfouling it.
▶ Don't dive under the boat in rough water conditions.

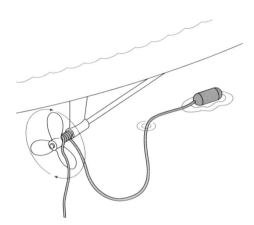

A line trailing from the boat or from a fish trap can wrap around the spinning shaft. The propeller stops turning because the line jams the shaft in place.

# ENGINE FAILURE

Prepare for engine failure by thinking of how you would control the boat in situations where you might lose power. Your action plan should include at least three steps: assess the situation; ensure the safety of the crew; and maximize your response options.

If you intend to set sail, remember that the wind will blow the bow down and unfurling the jib may be the best option. Once steerage is regained, head up to a close reach and then raise the main.

| Situation | Response |
| --- | --- |
| **Open water** | Set sail, heave-to or drift. Troubleshoot the engine. |
| **Busy channel** | Set sail or drift to the edge of a channel. Anchor clear of traffic. Intentional grounding in a safe area is a viable option. |
| **Close quarters** | Rig fenders and drift or sail to a dock, moor or anchor, or raft to a moored boat. |
| **Lee shore** | Anchor immediately. If anchoring is not feasible, set sail. |

# STEERING FAILURE

If you have a steering failure, the emergency tiller provides a backup. Know where the emergency tiller is stowed, and keep the tools needed for installation with it. Practice installing it before leaving the dock. Attaching the tiller may require removal of the wheel.

If your steering quadrant or cable breaks while underway in open water, trim the sails to maintain your course while you complete the emergency installation.

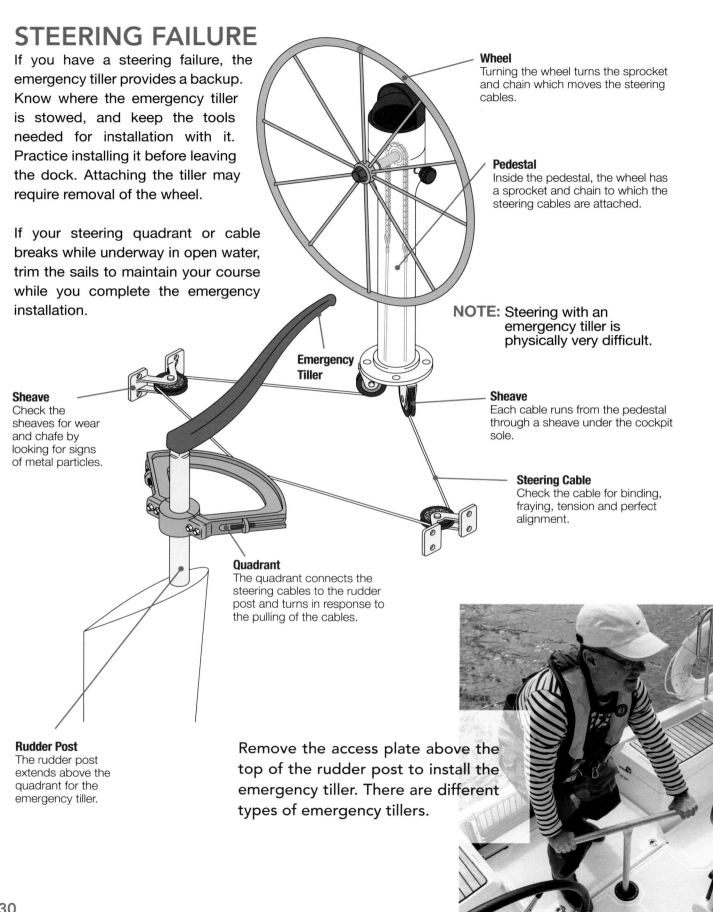

**Wheel**
Turning the wheel turns the sprocket and chain which moves the steering cables.

**Pedestal**
Inside the pedestal, the wheel has a sprocket and chain to which the steering cables are attached.

**NOTE:** Steering with an emergency tiller is physically very difficult.

**Emergency Tiller**

**Sheave**
Check the sheaves for wear and chafe by looking for signs of metal particles.

**Sheave**
Each cable runs from the pedestal through a sheave under the cockpit sole.

**Steering Cable**
Check the cable for binding, fraying, tension and perfect alignment.

**Quadrant**
The quadrant connects the steering cables to the rudder post and turns in response to the pulling of the cables.

**Rudder Post**
The rudder post extends above the quadrant for the emergency tiller.

Remove the access plate above the top of the rudder post to install the emergency tiller. There are different types of emergency tillers.

# FREEING A GROUNDED BOAT

Sooner or later all sailors run aground. What you do next, and how rapidly you do it, depends on the circumstances.

First check for injured crew and see if you are taking on water. If there are no injuries, no damage to the boat, and the tide is rising, just waiting may be your best option.

The diagrams on this page provide more active methods of freeing a grounded boat.

## BACKING OFF UNDER POWER

Attempt to back off under power. Hold the wheel firmly so the rudder isn't forced hard over and damaged as sternway increases. Bring the rpms up slowly. Watch for excessive mud and debris which can be pulled into your raw water cooling system.

## HEELING THE BOAT

Decrease the boat's draft by heeling it. Having the crew sit on the boom may free the keel from the bottom. First, swing the boom out to one side and secure it with a preventer. Use a line from aloft to reinforce the topping lift. Have the crew slide onto the boom.

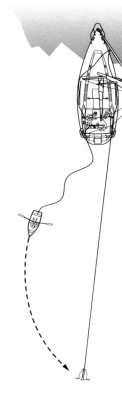

## KEDGING

If simple means like backing off under power or heeling the boat have failed to refloat the boat, the next logical step is kedging the boat off. Use your dinghy to carry the anchor into deep water until you reach a scope of 5:1 or more. Lead the anchor rode to your windlass or largest winch and grind it in. Secure the rudder so that it will not be damaged if the boat will be moving backward. If you have no dinghy, float the anchor with life jackets and swim it out.

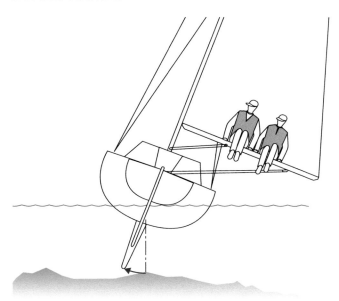

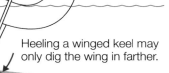

Heeling a winged keel may only dig the wing in farther.

131

# FLOODING

Water entering the boat needs to be dealt with quickly. A 1½" hole two feet below the waterline line will let approximately 70 gallons of water per minute into your boat. Most manual bilge pumps are rated at no more than 20 gallons a minute. Electric pumps, many with higher capacities, will only work until the water reaches the batteries. Broadcast a **PAN-PAN** or a **MAYDAY**. They can always be canceled later.

Common causes of water in the bilge are an open head valve, a water hose that has detached, a leaking water tank, shower sump overflow, leaking hatches and heeling.

If the leak wasn't caused by a collision, check pressure water faucets in the heads and galley. Shut off freshwater and saltwater pumps. Check for an overflowing head, an open hatch, overflow from the shower sump, or a leaking stuffing box. The water may be coming in through one of the through-hull fittings below the waterline, which are equipped with seacocks. Close all the seacocks and pump out the water. If the source of the water is not obvious, reopen the seacocks one at a time to find the source of the leak. All boats should be equipped with tapered wooden plugs that can be driven into a detached hose, broken through-hull fitting or seacock. Another possibility is a leaking water tank (in which case the flood water will be fresh, not salty and you are not sinking).

If you have been holed, heel the boat to elevate the hole close to or above the waterline. Plug the hole with anything available (e.g., clothing, sails, cushions). Ideally, you would like to seal the hole, but slowing the flooding so that the pumps can keep up may be your best option.

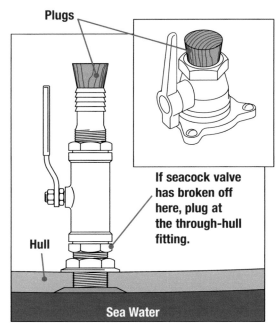

Flooding may happen if a through-hull fitting breaks, in which case you should pound a tapered wooden plug into the hole.

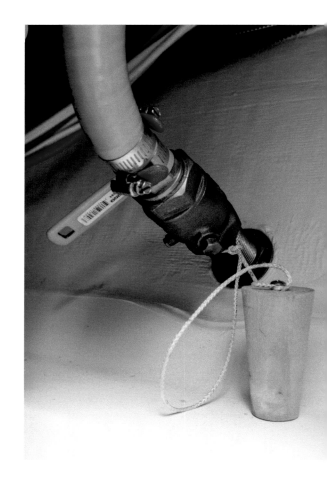

### Dos and Don'ts
▶ Do tell everyone to put on a life jacket.
▶ Don't abandon ship unless there are NO other alternatives.
▶ Do maneuver the boat to shallow water or a safe harbor. Intentionally grounding the boat may be the safest way to save the crew and later the boat.
▶ Do follow charter company procedures.

# SINKING

Abandon ship only if your boat is sinking and you have no alternatives. A small raft is much harder to find at sea than a boat. If a vessel is not already standing by, issue a Mayday call, giving your location and number of crew. If your boat has no life raft, you will have to use the dinghy. Attempt to keep crew and gear as dry as possible when transferring from the boat.

## DISTRESS SIGNALS

Flares fired from a pistol or launcher are visible over the horizon day or night. Hand-held flares can pinpoint your location for rescuers, but should be used with great caution around a rubber raft. The U.S. Coast Guard requires vessels over 16 feet to have three daylight and three night flares or three combination daylight/night devices readily available, none of which have expired. Sound horns and bells continuously. Use your flashlight or radio to send the international distress signal SOS.

**SOS**

The Emergency Position-Indicating Radio Beacon (EPIRB) issues a signal to satellites and aircraft when activated. Use only in extreme emergencies.

### ACTION PLAN CHECKLIST

▶ Notify everyone that it's time to abandon ship and make sure they are wearing warm clothes and a life jacket.
▶ Assign each crew a task:
  • Tie the life raft to a structural part of the boat and deploy it overboard.
  • Activate the EPIRB.
  • Send Mayday on VHF.
  • Fire flares.
  • Get food, water, medication(s) and ID.
▶ Take EPIRB and hand-held VHF radio with you.
▶ Get into life raft.
▶ Cut painter when everyone is accounted for.

### SAFETY TIPS FOR DISTRESS FLARES

▶ Hold a flare gun or a hand-held meteor launcher firmly over your head. They have a noticeable recoil and hot bits will fly out of the muzzle.
▶ It is not always clear how to light hand-held locater flares and smoke signals. Take a moment to read the directions before you need them.
▶ Hand-held locater flares drip hot slag and must be held over the downwind side of the boat. When they go out, drop them in the water.

## DEPLOYING A LIFE RAFT

**1** Tie off the painter to the structural part of boat. Keep a knife handy to cut the painter, if necessary.

**2** Tell the strongest crew member to push or throw the canister or valise into the water.

**3** Pull out the painter to activate $CO_2$ inflation.

**4** Transfer crew and gear into the life raft.

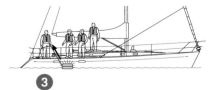 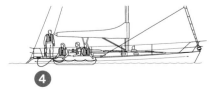

# TROUBLESHOOTING

If you can diagnose common problems that occur in boat systems, you will be better able to coordinate repairs with your charter company. Beyond spare coolant and oil, the charter company commonly does not provide many tools or spare parts. Charter companies prefer to make repairs themselves.

## ENGINE

▶ If the engine turns over but won't run, make sure the engine stop control is in the RUN position.

▶ If engine alarm sounds while running under power, check temperature and oil pressure gauges, lights and the exhaust for water. Stop the engine. Make sure the raw water intake is open and clear and the raw water filter is clean.

▶ If the engine overheats and the alternator doesn't charge, check the alternator and raw water pump belts for tight fit.

▶ If the control cables break, it may be possible to operate the controls from the engine.

▶ If the oil in the engine looks like chocolate milk, salt water is getting into the engine. Do not start engine and call the charter company.

▶ If you smell diesel exhaust in the cabin, check to see if there's a hole in the exhaust system.

## STEERING

▶ If it's hard to turn the wheel, loosen the wheel brake.

▶ If the steering wheel feels unresponsive, make sure the cable is tight and hasn't jumped the quadrant.

▶ If the steering cable breaks, sail to balance before rigging the emergency tiller.

▶ If you see metal filings under the steering sheaves or quadrant, check for a binding cable.

## ELECTRICAL

▶ If the batteries don't accept a charge or they discharge too quickly, check the alternator belt tension and battery water level. Check the connections and terminals on the batteries.

▶ The electrical usage should be monitored, and it may be necessary to charge the batteries longer.

▶ If electrical items (e.g., fans, lights, stove, windlass) do not work, check the circuit breakers on the electrical panel and all switches.

## REFRIGERATION

▶ If the unit runs continuously, the contents do not stay cold, and the ice melts too soon, make sure the box is securely closed and check the thermostat setting.

▶ If the refrigeration is engine-driven and the refrigerator doesn't stay cold, run the engine longer or more often.

## HEAD

▶ If water doesn't pump into the bowl, check that the intake seacock is open and that the valve is in the flush (wet) position.

▶ If it is hard to pump, check the holding tank, as it may be full.

▶ If the head is clogged, it is best to call the charter company.

## FRESH WATER

▶ A constantly running pressure water pump may indicate a leak in the system or an empty water tank that could burn out the pump.

135

# GLOSSARY OF SAILING TERMS

Including radio/signal flag terms (in parenthesis)

## A (Alpha)

**Abeam** - off the side of (at right angle to) the boat
**Aft** - at or toward the stern or behind the boat
**Alternator** - a device which generates electricity from an engine
**Amidships** - toward the center of the boat
**Apparent wind** - the wind aboard a moving boat
**Astern** - behind the stern of the boat
**Athwartships** - across the boat from side to side

## B (Bravo)

**Back** - (1) to hold the clew of a sail out to windward; (2) a counterclockwise change of wind direction
**Back and fill** - using forward and reverse gears, as well as an inboard engine's prop walk and rudder angles, to turn a boat in close quarters
**Backstay** - the standing rigging running from the stern to the top of the mast
**Ballast** - weight in the keel that provides stability
**Barometer** - a weather forecasting instrument that measures air pressure
**Batten** - a thin slat that slides into a pocket in the leech of a sail, helping it hold its shape
**Battery switch** - the main electrical cut-off switch
**Beam** - the width of a boat at its widest point
**Beam reach (point of sail)** - sailing in a direction at approximately 90 degrees to the wind
**Bear away** - to fall off, head away from the wind
**Bearing** - the direction from one object to another expressed in compass degrees
**Beating** - a course sailed upwind
**Below** - the area of a boat beneath the deck
**Bend** - (1) to attach a sail to a spar or a headstay; (2) to attach a line to a sail
**Berth** - (1) the area in which you park your boat; (2) the area in which you sleep on a boat
**Bight** - part of a line doubled back onto itself
**Bilge** - the lowest part of the boat's interior where water on board will collect
**Bimini top** - a sun awning used to cover the cockpit area
**Bitter end** - the end of a line
**Blanket** - to use a sail or an object to block the wind from filling a sail
**Block** - a pulley on a boat
**Boat hook** - a pole with a hook used for grabbing hold of a mooring or an object in the water
**Bolt rope** - the rope sewn into the foot and luff of some mainsails and the luff of some jibs by which the sails are attached to the boat
**Boom vang** - a block and tackle system which pulls the boom down to assist sail control
**Bow** - the forward part of the boat
**Bow line (BOW-line)** - a line running from the bow of the boat to the dock or mooring
**Bowline (BOE-lin)** - a knot designed to make a loop that will not slip and can be easily untied
**Breast line** - a short dock line leading off the beam of the boat directly to the dock
**Broach** - to round up uncontrollably while going downwind
**Broad reach** - sailing at an angle away from the wind

**Bulkhead** - a wall that runs athwartships on a boat, usually providing structural support to the hull
**By the lee** - sailing on a run with the wind coming over the same side of the boat as the boom

## C (Charlie)

**Cabin** - the interior of a boat
**Can** - an odd-numbered, green buoy marking the left side of a channel when returning to port
**Cast off** - to release a line
**Center of effort** - the focal point of the force of the wind on the sails
**Center of lateral resistance** - the focal point of the force of the water on the underbody of the boat
**Centerline** - the midline of a boat running from bow to stern
**Chafe** - wear on a line caused by rubbing
**Chainplates** - strong metal plates that connect the shrouds to the boat
**Channel** - a (usually narrow) path in the water, marked by buoys, in which the water is deep enough to sail
**Chart** - a nautical map
**Charter** - to rent a boat
**Chock** - a guide mounted on the deck through which dock lines and anchor rode are run
**Choke** - a device for controlling the mixture of air and fuel for a gasoline engine
**Chop** - rough, short, steep waves
**Clew** - the lower, aft corner of a sail
**Close-hauled** - the point of sail closest to the wind
**Close-reach** - the point of sail in a direction with the wind forward of the beam, but aft of the close-hauled position
**Coaming** - the short wall surrounding the cockpit
**Cockpit** - the lower area in which the sail controls are located
**Coil** - to loop a line neatly so it can be stored
**Come about** - *see* Tack
**Companionway** - the steps leading from the cockpit or deck to the cabin below
**Compass** - the magnetic instrument that indicates the direction in which the boat is headed
**Compass protractor** - a plotting instrument oriented to latitude-longitude lines
**Compass rose** - the circle(s) on a chart that indicates the direction of true north and magnetic north
**Compressed Natural Gas (CNG)** - a cooking fuel
**Converter** - a device to change AC current to DC
**Course** - the direction in which the boat is steered
**Courtesy flag** - the national flag of a host country
**Cowl** - a ventilator funnel on deck
**Crew** - besides the skipper, anyone on board
**Cringle** - a ring sewn or pressed into a corner or edge of a sail
**Cunningham** - a line running through a grommet near the tack of a mainsail used to tighten the luff
**Current** - the horizontal movement of water caused by tides, wind and other forces

## D (Delta)

**Dead downwind** - sailing in a direction straight downwind
**Deck plate** - a covered opening on deck leading to the water, fuel or holding tanks, or for access to the rudder post
**Depower** - to release the power from the sails by allowing them to luff or become flatter
**Dinghy** - a small, open boat often used as a tender to a larger boat

**Displacement** - the weight of a boat; therefore, the amount of water it displaces

**Divider** - an instrument used for measuring distances or coordinates on a chart

**Dock** - (1) the wooden structure where a boat may be tied up; (2) the act of bringing the boat to rest alongside the structure

**Dock line** - a line used to secure the boat to the dock

**Dodger** - a canvas protection in front of the cockpit designed to keep spray off the skipper and crew

**Dog** - (1) screw-type latches on ports; (2) to fasten a port or hatch securely

**Dorade vent** - a cowled box vent that lets air into the boat without letting in water

**Downhaul** - a line used to tighten the luff of a mainsail by pulling down on a movable gooseneck

**Downwind** - away from the direction of the wind

**Draft** - the depth of a boat from the water's surface

## E (Echo)

**Ease** - to let out a line or sail

**Ebb** - an outgoing current associated with a falling tide

**Emergency Position-Indicating Radio Beacon (EPIRB)** - used to alert search and rescue services in the event of an emergency

## F (Foxtrot)

**Fairlead** - a fitting that guides a jib sheet or other lines back to the cockpit or along the deck

**Fairway** - a clear path on the water where vessels may not anchor and structures are not placed

**Fake** - to lay out a line on deck using large loops to prevent tangling

**Fall off** - *see* Head down

**Fast** - secured

**Fathom** - a measurement of the depth of water; one fathom equals six feet

**Feathering** - sailing closer to the wind to depower

**Feathering propeller** - a propeller with blades that align with the water flow

**Fender** - a device used to protect a boat's hull when coming alongside

**Fetch** - (1) *see* Lay; (2) a distance of open water between a shore and a position over which waves build up

**Fitting** - a piece of nautical hardware

**Float plan** - an itinerary of your intended sailing trip that is left onshore with a responsible party

**Float switch** - a device that turns on the bilge pump when water inside the boat reaches a certain height

**Flood** - an incoming current associated with a rising tide

**Flotilla** - a group of boats on an organized cruise

**Following sea** - waves hitting the boat from astern

**Foot** - the bottom edge of a sail

**Fore** - forward

**Forepeak** - a below-the-deck storage area in the bow

**Foresail** - a jib or a genoa

**Forestay** - the standing rigging running from the bow to the mast on which the jib is hanked

**Forward** - toward the bow

**Fouled** - tangled

**Freeboard** - the height of the hull above the water's surface

**Full** - not luffing

**Furl** - to fold or roll up a sail

## G (Golf)

**Genoa** - a large jib whose clew extends aft of the mast

**Gimbal** - a pivot that allows the stove to remain horizontal when the boat is heeling

**Give-way vessel** - the vessel required to change course when on a collision course with another boat

**Glide zone** - the distance a sailboat takes to coast to a stop

**Gooseneck** - the strong fitting that connects the boom to the mast

**Grommet** - a reinforcing metal ring set in a sail

**Ground tackle** - the anchor and rode (chain and line)

**Gunwale (GUN-nle)** - the edge of the deck where it meets the topside

## H (Hotel)

**Halyard** - a line used to hoist or lower a sail

**Hank** - a snap hook that is used to connect the luff of a jib onto the forestay

**Hard alee** - the command given to the crew just prior to tacking

**Hard over** - to turn the tiller or wheel as far as possible in one direction

**Harness** - *see* Safety harness

**Hatch** - a large covered opening in the deck

**Hatch boards** - boards that close off the companionway

**Haul in** - to tighten a line

**Head** - (1) the top corner of a sail; (2) the bathroom on a boat; (3) the toilet on a boat

**Head down** - to change course away from the wind

**Head off** - *see* Head down

**Head up** - to change course toward the wind

**Headboard** - the reinforcing small board affixed to the head of a sail

**Header** - a wind shift that makes your boat head down or requires that sails be sheeted in

**Heading** - the direction of the boat expressed in compass degrees

**Headsail** - a jib, genoa or staysail

**Headstay** - the standing rigging running from the bow to the mast

**Head-to-wind** - the course of the boat when the bow is dead into the wind

**Headway** - forward progress

**Heave-to** - to hold one's position in the water by using the rudder and the force of the sails to counter one another

**Heavy weather** - strong winds and large waves

**Heel** - the lean of a boat caused by the wind

**Helm** - the tiller or wheel

**Helmsman** - the person responsible for steering

**Holding ground** - the bottom ground in an anchorage used to hold the anchor

**Holding tank** - a tank used to store toilet waste until it can be properly disposed of

**Hove-to** - a boat that has completed the process of heaving-to, with its jib aback, its main loosely trimmed, and its rudder securely positioned to steer it close to the wind

**Hull speed** - the theoretical maximum speed of a sailboat determined by the length of its waterline

## I (India)

**In irons** - a boat stopped head to wind

**Inboard** - inside of the rail of a boat

**Inverter** - a device to change DC current to AC

**Isobar** - a line joining places of equal air pressure as depicted on weather maps

## J (Juliet)

**Jacklines** - sturdy wire, rope or webbing securely fastened at its ends on deck that permits the crew to hook in with their safety harnesses

**Jib** - the small forward sail attached to the forestay

**Jibe** - to change tacks by turning the stern through the wind

**Jiffy reef** - a quick reefing system allowing a section of the mainsail to be tied to the boom

**Jury rig** - an improvised, temporary repair

## K (Kilo)

**Kedge off** - to use an anchor to pull a boat into deeper water after it has run aground

**Keel** - the heavy vertical fin beneath a boat that helps keep it upright and prevents it from slipping sideways in the water

**Kill switch** - engine stop control

**King spoke** - a marker on the steering wheel that indicates when the rudder is centered

**Knockdown** - a boat heeled so far that one of its spreaders touches the water

**Knot** - one nautical mile per hour

## L (Lima)

**Land breeze** - a wind blowing over land and out to sea

**Lash** - to tie down

**Lay** - to sail a course that will clear an obstacle without tacking

**Lazarette** - a storage compartment under the after deck

**Lazy sheet** - the windward side jib sheet that is not under strain

**Lead (LEED)** - to pass a line through a fitting or block

**Lee helm** - the boat's tendency to turn away from the wind

**Lee shore** - land that is on the leeward side of the boat; because the wind is blowing in that direction, a lee shore could pose a danger.

**Leech** - the after edge of a sail

**Leech line** - an adjustable cord sewn into the back edge of a sail to prevent fluttering

**Leeward (LEW-erd)** - the direction away from the wind (where the wind is blowing to)

**Leeward side** - the side of the boat or sail that is away from the wind

**Leeway** - sideways slippage of the boat in a direction away from the wind

**Life jacket** - a sleeveless buoyant or inflatable jacket for keeping a person afloat in water

**Lifeline** - plastic coated wire, supported by stanchions, around the outside of the deck to help prevent crew members from falling overboard

**Lifesling** - a floating device attached to the boat by a length of floating line that doubles as a hoisting sling to retrieve a person in the water

**Lift** - (1) the force that results from air passing by a sail, or water past a keel, that moves the boat forward and sideways; (2) a change in wind direction that lets the boat head up

**Line** - a nautical rope

**Line stoppers** - levered cleats that hold lines under load and can be easily released

**Lubber's line** - a small post in a compass used to help determine a course or a bearing

**Luff** - (1) the forward edge of a sail; (2) the fluttering of a sail caused by aiming too close to the wind

## M (Mike)

**Magnetic** - in reference to magnetic north rather than true north

**Mainmast** - the tallest mast on a boat

**Marine Sanitation Device (MSD)** - includes head, holding tank and connecting lines and valves

**Marlinspike** - a pointed tool used to loosen knots

**Mast step** - the structure on which the bottom of the mast sits

**Master switch** - *see* Battery switch

**Masthead** - the top of the mast

**Masthead fly** - a wind direction indicator on top of the mast

**Mayday** - the internationally recognized distress signal for a life-threatening emergency

**Mooring** - a permanently anchored ball or buoy to which a boat can be tied

## N (November)

**Nautical mile** - a distance of 6076 feet, equaling one minute of the earth's latitude

**Navigation Rules** - laws established to prevent collisions on the water

**No-Go Zone** - an area into the wind in which a boat cannot produce power to sail

**Nun** - a red, even-numbered buoy, marking the right side of a channel when returning to port; nuns are usually paired with cans

## O (Oscar)

**Off the wind** - sailing downwind

**Offshore** - away from or out of sight of land

**Offshore wind** - wind blowing away from the land

**On the wind** - sailing upwind, close-hauled

**Outboard** - (1) a portable engine mounted on the transom; (2) a position away from the centerline of the boat

**Outhaul** - the controlling line attached to the clew of a mainsail used to tension the foot of the sail

**Overpowered** - a boat that is heeling too far because it has too much sail up for the amount of wind

**Overtaking** - a boat that is catching up to another boat and about to pass it

## P (Papa)

**Packing gland** - *see* Stuffing box

**Painter** - the line attached to the bow of a dinghy

**Pan-Pan** - the internationally recognized distress signal for an urgent, but not life-threatening, situation

**Parallel rulers** - two rulers linked and held parallel by hinges used to plot a course

**Pasarelle** - used in Med Mooring, a plank or gangway connecting the transom to a dock or quay

**Pay out** - to ease a line

**Pendant** - added length of wire or line used on mooring buoys, also used on sails to lengthen hoist

**Person In Water (PIW)** - a term used by a water rescue team

**Piling** - vertical timber or log driven into the sea bottom to support docks or form a breakwater

**Pinching** - sailing too close to the wind

**Plot** - applying calculations to a chart to determine course or position

**Point** - to steer close to the wind

**Points of sail** - boat directions in relation to wind direction (e.g., close-hauled, beam reaching, broad reaching and running)

**Port** - (1) the left side of a boat when facing forward; (2) a harbor; (3) a window in a cabin on a boat

**Port tack** - sailing on any point of sail with the main boom on the starboard side of the boat

**Prevailing wind** - typical or consistent wind conditions

**Propane** - a cooking fuel

**Propeller** - a device, having a revolving hub with radiating blades, that is used for propulsion

**Puff** - an increase in wind speed for a short duration

**Pulpit** - a stainless steel guardrail at the bow and stern of some boats

**Pumpout station** - location for legal emptying of holding tanks

**Pushpit** - a stainless steel guardrail at the stern of some boats

## Q (Quebec)

**Q flag** - a rectangular yellow flag shown on arrival in a foreign country indicating that the boat has not yet completed entrance formalities

**Quadrant** - connects the rudder post to the steering cables in wheel steering

**Quarter** - the sides of the boat near the stern

**Quarter berth** - a bunk located under the cockpit

## R (Romeo)

**Radar reflector** - a metal device designed to effectively reflect radar and make the boat more visible on other boats' radars

**Rake** - the angle of the mast

**Range** - the alignment of two objects that indicates the middle of a channel

**Raw water** - water from outside the boat brought in through hoses for engine cooling or toilet flushing

**Reach** - one of several points of sail across the wind

**Ready about** - the command given to the crew to prepare to tack

**Ready to jibe** - the command given to the crew to prepare to jibe

**Reef** - to reduce the size of a sail

**Reefing line** - a line used to reduce sail by pulling the lower portion of the sail to the boom

**Reeve** - to pass a line through a cringle or block

**Rhumb line** - a straight course between two points

**Rig** - (1) the design of a boat's mast(s), standing rigging and sail plan; (2) to prepare a boat to go sailing

**Rigging** - the wires and lines used to support and control sails

**Right-of-way** - the right of the stand-on vessel to hold its course

**Roach** - the sail area aft of a straight line running from the head to the clew of a sail

**Rode** - line and chain attached from the boat to the anchor

**Roller furling** - a mechanical system to roll up a headsail (jib) around the headstay

**Round up** - when the boat turns, sometimes abruptly and with a great deal of heel, towards the wind

**Rudder** - the underwater fin that is controlled by the wheel or tiller to deflect water and steer the boat

**Run** - point of sail, sailing with the wind coming behind the boat

**Running rigging** - lines and hardware used to control the sails

## S (Sierra)

**Safety harness** - a harness worn by crew members and attached to the boat by a tether to prevent crew members from falling overboard

**Sail ties** - pieces of line or webbing used to tie the mainsail to the boom when reefing or storing the sail

**Scope** - the ratio of the amount of anchor rode deployed to the distance from the bow to the bottom

**Scull** - to propel a boat by swinging the rudder back and forth like a fish tail

**Scupper** - cockpit or deck drain

**Sea breeze** - a wind that blows over the sea and onto the land

**Seabag** - a soft fabric bag for carrying personal items

**Seacock** - a valve attached to the hull, which shuts off hoses through which raw water is brought into the boat

**Secure** - to make safe or cleat

**Sécurité** - an internationally recognized signal to warn others of a dangerous situation

**Set** - (1) the direction of a current; (2) to trim the sails

**Shackle** - a metal fitting at the end of a line used to attach the line to a sail or another fitting

**Shake out** - to remove a reef and restore the full sail

**Sheave** - the rotating wheel inside a block or fitting

**Sheet** - the line that is used to control the sail by easing it out or trimming it in

**Shoal** - shallow water that may be dangerous

**Shroud** - standing rigging at the side of the mast

**S-jibe** - the controlled method of jibing with the mainsail crossing the boat under control and the boat's path making an s-shaped course

**Skeg** - a vertical fin in front of the rudder

**Skipper** - the person in charge of the boat

**Slab reefing (jiffy reefing)** - lowering and tying off the lower portion of a sail in order to reduce sail area

**Slip** - see Berth

**Snub** - to hold a line under tension by wrapping it on a winch or cleat

**Sole** - the floor in a cockpit or cabin

**Solenoid switch** - an electrical switch that shuts off the flow of propane

**Spar** - a pole used to attach a sail on a boat (e.g., mast, boom, gaff)

**Spinnaker** - a large billowing headsail used when sailing downwind

**Splice** - the joining of two lines together by interweaving their strands

**Spreader** - a support strut extending athwartships from the mast used to support the mast and guide the shrouds from the top of the mast to the chainplates

**Spring line** - a dock line running forward or aft from the boat to the dock to keep the boat from moving forward or aft

**Squall** - a short intense storm with little warning

**Stanchions** - stainless steel supports at the edge of the deck that hold the lifelines

**Standing rigging** - the permanent rigging (usually wire) of a boat, including the forestay, backstay and shrouds

**Stand-on vessel** - the vessel or boat with the right-of-way

**Starboard** - the right side of the boat facing forward

**Starboard tack** - sailing on any point of sail with the main boom on the port side of the boat

**Stay** - a wire support for a mast, part of the standing rigging

**Staysail (STAY-sil)** - on a cutter, a second small "inner jib" that is attached between the bow and the mast

**Steerageway** - the minimum amount of speed needed to control the direction of a vessel

**Stem** - the forward tip of the bow

**Step** - the area in which the base of the mast fits

**Stern** - the aft part of the boat

**Stuffing box** - the opening in the hull where the propeller shaft exits

**Sump** - a cavity or tank in the bilge to collect water

## T (Tango)

**Tack** - (1) a course on which the wind comes over one side of the boat (e.g., port tack, starboard tack); (2) to change tacks by turning the bow through the wind; (3) the lower forward corner of a sail

**Tackle** - a sequence of blocks and line that provides a mechanical advantage

**Tail** - to hold and pull a line from behind a winch

**Telltales** - pieces of yarn or sailcloth material attached to sails that indicate when the sail is properly trimmed

**Tether** - length of line connecting a safety harness to a padeye or jackline

**Throttle** - a device used for controlling the engine's revolutions per minute (RPM)

**Tide** - the rise and fall of the water level due to the gravitational pull of the sun and moon

**Toe rail** - a short aluminum or wooden rail around the outer edges of the deck

**Topping lift** - a line used to hold the boom up when the mainsail is lowered or stowed

**Topsides** - the sides of the boat between the waterline and the deck

**Transom** - the vertical surface of the stern

**Traveler** - a track or bridle that controls sideways (athwartships) movement of the mainsail

**Trim** - (1) to pull in on a sheet; (2) how a sail is set relative to the wind

**True wind** - the actual speed and direction of the wind when standing still

**Tune** - to adjust a boat's standing rigging

**Turnbuckle** - a screw device attached to the lower end of standing rigging which permits adjustment of the tension on the wire

## U (Uniform)

**Underway** - not anchored, aground, or made fast to the shore

**Upwind** - toward the direction of the wind

**USCG** - abbreviation for United States Coast Guard

## V (Victor)

**Vang** - *see* Boom vang

**V-berth** - a bunk in the bow of the boat that narrows as it goes forward

**Veer** - a clockwise change of wind direction

**Very High Frequency (VHF)** - a two-way radio commonly used for boating

**Vessel** - any sailboat, powerboat or ship

## W (Whiskey)

**Wake** - waves caused by a boat moving through water

**Warping** - to move a vessel by hauling on a line made fast to a dock, piling, anchor, pier or other stationary object

**Waterline** - the line on the hull at which the boat sits in the water

**Weather helm** - the boat's tendency to head up toward the wind, which occurs when a sailboat is overpowered or the sail trim is out of balance (i.e., jib trim is too loose and/or mainsail trim is too tight)

**Weather side** - *see* Windward side

**Whip** - to bind together the strands at the end of a line

**Whisker pole** - a pole, temporarily mounted between the mast and the clew of a jib, used to hold the jib out and keep it full when sailing downwind

**White caps** - waves with foam tops

**Winch** - a drum with a handle offering mechanical advantage to trim sheets or raise sails

**Windage** - the amount of surface area, including sails, rigging and hull, that is presented to the wind

**Windward** - toward the wind

**Windward side** - the side of a boat or a sail closest to the wind

**Wing-and-wing** - sailing downwind with the jib set on the opposite side of the mainsail

**Working sails** - the mainsail and standard jib

**Working sheet** - the leeward jib sheet that is tensioned by the wind on the sail

## X (Xray)

## Y (Yankee)

**Y-valve** - a double valve used to redirect water flow

## Z (Zulu)

# US Sailing Bareboat Cruising Certification

The Bareboat Cruising graduate will have successfully demonstrated the ability to skipper and crew an inboard auxiliary powered cruising sailboat within sight of land and bring it safely to anchor during daylight hours.

**Recommended Equipment:** It is recommended that Bareboat Cruising courses and examinations be conducted on 30' to 45' sloop-rigged cruising keelboats with wheel steering and auxiliary diesel power, and with adequate equipment inventory to complete all required certification outcomes.

**Prerequisite:** The prerequisite for Bareboat Cruising Certification is a US Sailing Basic Cruising Certification.

**Certification Requirements:** Bareboat Cruising Certification requires the successful completion of the following knowledge and skill requirements. These requirements are expected to be able to be performed safely with confident command of the boat with a wind of at least 15 knots.

## Practical Skills

### Preparation to Sail

1. Obtain an appropriate weather forecast for your cruise and plan accordingly.
2. Check the sail inventory and select the appropriate sails for the conditions.
3. Check the location and condition or operation of all safety equipment.
4. Describe the need to be aware of and perform checks of the engine fluids and mechanical parts, manual and electric bilge pumps, and the electrical, mechanical, fresh water, marine head and holding tank systems.
5. Perform a complete check and demonstrate safe use of the galley stove and stove fuel system.
6. Ensure that all necessary provisions, cooking and eating utensils are aboard and properly stowed.
7. Check the security and operation of all hatches, ports and companionways.
8. Inventory and check the condition of all bimini tops, cockpit awnings and dodgers where applicable.
9. Inventory and check the condition of all tools and spare parts.
10. Check the condition of dinghy and oars (and outboard, if applicable).
11. Inventory and check the condition of all required charts, tide tables, cruising guides and navigation tools.
12. Perform a complete inspection of all deck gear: standing and running rigging; lifelines; stanchions; and pulpits.
13. Understand your responsibilities and liabilities as a bareboat charter customer according to your contract with your charter company.

### Crew Operations and Skills

14. Demonstrate a comprehensive crew briefing and plan of responsibilities.
15. Demonstrate the operation of the emergency steering equipment.

### Leaving the Dock or Mooring

16. Demonstrate the proper lashing of a dinghy on deck or securing it for towing.
17. Demonstrate appropriate helmsman and crew coordination and the skills necessary for leaving under power in any wind condition.

### Navigation

18. Demonstrate your ability to: correctly use a handbearing compass and a ship's compass; maintain a proper DR plot with time/speed/distance calculations; plot a fix using lines of position and/or ranges; use depth sounder; use accepted plotting and labeling techniques; understand buoyage systems and aids to navigation; identify and correlate visual observations and landmarks with chart symbols.
19. Use a GPS chart plotter to plan and sail a multi-leg route.

### Heavy Weather Sailing

20. Demonstrate shortening sail to depower, and explain effects on balancing the boat.
21. Demonstrate heaving-to.

### Overboard Rescue Methods

22. Properly demonstrate one of the overboard rescue methods under sail, which is most appropriate for: your sailing ability; boat type; crew experience; wind and sea conditions; and maintaining constant visual contact with the person in water.
23. Demonstrate an overboard rescue method under power which allows you to maintain visual contact with the person in water.

### Anchoring Techniques

24. Select an anchorage and demonstrate appropriate helmsman and crew coordination and the skills necessary to anchor with two anchors under power using one of the following methods: bow and stern; two anchors off the bow at 60 degrees; or two anchors off the bow at 180 degrees (Bahamian Moor).
25. Pick up a mooring.
26. Demonstrate appropriate helmsman and crew coordination and the skills necessary to recover your anchor under power.

## Returning to the Dock or Mooring

27. Demonstrate appropriate helmsman and crew coordination and the skills necessary for returning to the dock under power in any wind direction.

## Securing the Boat Properly

28. Demonstrate the correct procedure for returning the charter boat in the same condition that it was chartered, and complete a charter check-in report on the condition of the boat.

# Knowledge

## Preparation to Sail

1. Understand bareboat charter procedures and responsibilities for both the charter company and the charter client.
2. Determine the vessel's fuel capacity, fuel consumption, and cruising range under power.
3. Be familiar with the documentation required for the vessel and crew, both nationally and internationally.
4. Be familiar with the legal responsibilities of a skipper and the courtesies to be observed when entering a foreign port.
5. Understand the legal responsibilities of the overboard discharge of pollutants.
6. Understand all federal, state and local regulations as they pertain to your boat.
7. Be familiar with all required documentation for crew and vessel nationally and internationally.

## Crew Operations and Skills

8. Be familiar with proper rafting techniques at docks and at anchor.

## Navigation

9. Understand how to: use tide and tidal current predictions; use the Rule of Twelfths; and apply set and drift and anticipated leeway when determining a course to steer.
10. Understand International Association of Marine Aids and Lighthouse Authorities (IALA) Systems A and B, including cardinal marks.
11. Be familiar with the considerations, responsibilities and special techniques required for navigation in restricted visibility.
12. Understand the meaning of the visual observations of water color.
13. Be familiar with the benefits and limitations of cruising guides.
14. Understand the Automatic Identification System (AIS).
15. Understand the limitations and potential dangers of electronic navigation.

## Heavy Weather Sailing

16. Describe the signs of an approaching squall and the actions to be taken.
17. Describe the desired orientation of the boat to the waves when heaving-to.

## Overboard Rescue Methods

18. Be familiar with the equipment provided for overboard rescue.
19. Understand procedures for overboard rescue in a larger cruising boat in unfamiliar waters and with a crew that you might not sail with regularly. Understand the Quick-Stop, Lifesling-type and Figure-8 overboard rescue methods under sail to include: constant visual contact with the person in water; communications; recovery plan; sequence of maneuvers; boat handling; course sailed; pickup approach; and coming alongside the person in water (or simulated object).
20. Describe methods of getting an overboard recovery person in water back on deck after the vessel is stopped alongside.
21. Explain when overboard rescue should be done under power and the inherent dangers.

## Safety and Emergency Procedures

22. Giving due consideration to the state of the tide, describe a plan of action if you run aground in moderate conditions.
23. Describe a plan of action if your vessel has: a broken through-hull; been holed; an engine failure; or a steering failure.

## Anchoring Techniques

24. Describe the procedures for anchoring with two anchors.
25. Describe the use of a trip line/anchor buoy.
26. Describe the procedures for clearing fouled anchor rodes, and for recovering an anchor from under another boat.
27. Describe the procedures for dealing with a dragging anchor.
28. Describe the advantages and disadvantages of the following anchoring methods: bow and stern; two anchors off the bow at 60 degrees; two anchors off the bow at 180 degrees (Bahamian Moor); and Mediterranean Moor.

## Returning to the Dock or Mooring

29. Describe the precautions when docking under sail.

## Securing the Boat Properly

30. Describe the responsibilities of the charter client and the charter company when returning the boat.

# What Can US Sailing Do for You?

US Sailing is committed to helping you discover and enjoy the beauty, relaxation, challenges and friendships of sailing. As part of this commitment we offer:

**KEELBOAT CERTIFICATION SYSTEM** with its various levels of training and certification:

**Basic Keelboat.** To responsibly skipper and crew a simple daysailing keelboat in familiar waters in light to moderate wind and sea conditions.

**Basic Cruising.** To responsibly skipper and crew an auxiliary powered cruising sailboat during daylight hours within sight of land in moderate wind and sea conditions.

**Bareboat Cruising.** To responsibly skipper, crew or bareboat charter an inboard auxiliary powered cruising sailboat within sight of land to a port or an anchorage during daylight hours in moderate to strong wind and sea conditions.

**Coastal Navigation.** To properly use traditional navigation techniques and electronic navigation for near coastal passage making.

**Coastal Passage Making.** To responsibly skipper and crew an inboard auxiliary powered cruising sailboat for coastal or offshore passages in strong to heavy conditions, including zero visibility and nighttime, in unfamiliar waters out of sight of land.

**Celestial Navigation.** To navigate using celestial techniques and integrating celestial with traditional navigation techniques.

**Cruising Catamaran Endorsement.** To responsibly skipper and crew on a cruising catamaran near shore with at least 10 knots of wind.

**Offshore Passage Making.** To responsibly skipper and crew an inboard auxiliary powered cruising sailboat to any destination worldwide.

**Performance Sailing.** To analyze, adjust and shape sails for maximum speed, and backstay and jib leads for optimum performance.

**SMALL BOAT CERTIFICATION SYSTEM** which is available for dinghy, daysailer and multihull sailors in two wind speed ranges: light and heavy air.

US Sailing certified instructors help you achieve new skills and knowledge using up-to-date and safe methods.

**PUBLICATIONS AND RESOURCES**

Course materials presented in a highly visual format to help you gain competency and confidence in your sailing skills and knowledge.

***The Official Logbook,*** recognized nationally, to document your US Sailing certifications and experience when chartering boats nationally.

**Website (ussailing.org)** of resources including an extensive list of accredited US Sailing schools that use both US Sailing certified instructors and US Sailing course materials.

**US Sailing Safety at Sea Courses**

**Racing Rules & Handicap Rating Systems**

**US Sailing membership** makes you a part of the National Governing Body for the Sport of Sailing and provides discounts on products and services that US Sailing offers.

**Notes**